How to Keep Your Children Safe

A Guide for Parents   Yvonne M. Vissing

How
to Keep
Your
Children
Safe

UNIVERSITY PRESS OF NEW ENGLAND

Hanover and London

Published by

University Press of New England,

One Court Street, Lebanon, NH 03766

www.upne.com

© 2006 by Yvonne Vissing

Printed in the United States of America

5 4 3 2 1

Library of Congress Cataloging-in-Publication Data

Vissing, Yvonne Marie.
How to keep your children safe : a guide for parents / Yvonne
M. Vissing.
       p.   cm.
Includes bibliographical references and index.
ISBN-13: 978-1-58465-529-9 (pbk. : alk. paper)
ISBN-10: 1-58465-529-1 (pbk. : alk. paper)
1. Child care—United States—Safety measures.
2. Children—Services for—United States—Safety measures.
3. Child abuse—United States—Prevention.
4. Children and adults—United States.
5. Safety education—United States. I. Title.
HQ778.63.V57 2006
649'.10289—dc22   2006026665

To Kiki,
Chris,
and
Leah

Contents

Preface

Parenting is one of the hardest responsibilities adults face. We do the best we can based on the experiences and resources we have, but sometimes we make mistakes that inadvertently put our children in harm's way. *How To Keep Your Children Safe* identifies areas of potential risk in an effort to help parents determine which people and situations are safe and which are not. What I learned through investigation is that the keys to quality care are no secret! They simply don't get conveyed to parents in ways that are readily accessible. *How To Keep Your Children Safe* takes a provocative look at child safety and recommends a proactive partnership approach for parents and caregivers.

The term "caregiver" in this book refers to anyone charged with the responsibility of ensuring the safety of children. It does not matter if caregivers are officially designated, and it does not matter if they are paid. Everyone may be put in the position of caregiver to other people's children at some time.

While Social Security is provided to support the elderly, there is no comprehensive care program to take care of our youngest citizens. Nearly every other industrialized country provides a more comprehensive national system of care and early education to children than the United States. I have discovered that quality care is often idiosyncratic rather than institutional. Lack of standards, policies, regulations, monitoring, and enforcement make quality care largely a matter of luck. A strong pro-child policy would help to protect kids. But parents have a responsibility to do things that will help keep their kids safe.

I recommend that a new covenant be created between social organizations, parents, and children. The government has a responsibility to provide funding and support to make children's well-being and safety a priority. Organizations have a responsibility to implement programs and policies that will ensure positive and healthy development for children. Parents need to actively seek out programs and care that will best meet their children's needs. They need to establish a trusting relationship and good communication with their children, so the children can tell them when they are scared, confused, worried, or upset. Sometimes children, especially those who are young or challenged, may not be able to articulate exactly what's going on in adult terminology. This means parents must look and listen carefully for signs of distress. If there are problems, children rely upon their parents to take responsible action. Communication by children is discouraged if they feel they will be blamed, get in trouble, or fear their parents will freak out when they confide about problems. Kids benefit when they know their parents will help.

This book takes a realistic look at everyday risks that confront children when they are away from their parents. It is also designed to give parents the information and support necessary to make good decisions. This book seeks to reassure parents that while good parenting is difficult, it is doable. The job of parenting is made easier when there is accurate information available. The actions recommended in this book are pragmatic and can be used by anyone to immediately change the course of life for their children for the better. This book will enlighten and empower parents, assist providers, and motivate communities to take better care of our children—our future.

Acknowledgments

I wish to extend sincere thanks to Phyllis Deutsch and the staff at the University Press of New England. Phyllis has been a tremendous source of encouragement and assistance during the production of this book. I also wish to thank Ellen Levine and her staff at the Trident Media Group for their support. Thanks are also given to the Sociology department and administration at Salem State College, with special thanks to Arthur Gould, Diane Lapkin, Anita Shea, and President Nancy Harrington. Thanks to John Patterson for his thoughtful comments, Mary Jane Moran for her insights on early child care safety, and to Nancy Berndtson for her assistance on clergy safety. Most importantly, I wish to thank my wonderful children for their love and patience. They have taught me how important it is that parents make sure their children are safe, and how parents have a responsibility to advocate for their kids even in difficult situations. This book is written so that other parents will have more information and so that their children will be safe, happy, and healthy. It is hoped that no parents will ever have to suffer the pain of losing children because the people who were supposed to protect them didn't. This book is written with a special remembrance of our friend, Thomas Nazarro.

Chapter 1 Are Kids Safe?

Life in contemporary American society requires that children spend considerable time in the care of "other people." These people include teachers, coaches, babysitters, camp counselors, ministers, neighbors, and friends, and most of the time the care children receive is of acceptable quality. But "acceptable care" lies on a continuum between "dangerous" and "wonderful." Parents are not usually aware of how much risk their children are in until something bad happens. Multiply all of the different types of caregiving situations by all of the potential risk factors, and it is enough to make any parent concerned. Parents assume that someone, somewhere, has evaluated all caregivers and found them to be safe, but in reality, this may not be the case. Children are put into at-risk situations because there is no comprehensive national commitment to ensure their safety. As a result, parents are responsible for deciding which caregivers are safe and which are not. Some parents rely on trust and assume that their children will be safe when they are with other people. Others, influenced by sensationalized media reports, have become so paranoid of what could happen that they do not let their children participate in normal social experiences. The decisions of all parents—those who do not worry enough and those who worry too much—impact the well-being of their children.

Realistically, a child can spend nearly half of his day with people other than his parents. These encounters run the gamut from brief interactions to intense, long-term relationships. Look at caregiving in a normal family: Maggie and Mark McCoy have two children: preschooler, Mary, and seventh-grader, Michael. Like most families, both parents are employed but still have to look at caregiving with both quality of care and dollar signs in mind. Mary needs someone to watch her for 35 hours a week for forty-eight out of fifty-two weeks a year (her parents have holiday or vacation time that make child care unnecessary four weeks a year), resulting in 1,680 hours of child care for Mary per year. When Maggie and Mark go to the movies or attend a funeral, they need a babysitter. Mary attends gymnastics, Sunday school, and visits a friend several times a month for an average of 6 hours a week for forty-eight weeks a year or an additional 288 hours a year. Thus, Mary spends 1,968 hours per year, or 34 percent of her waking time, in the care of another person. Now turn to Michael. The bus driver picks him up for school, where he's with fifty other kids for the twenty-minute ride. Since the McCoys don't get home from work until 5:30, he needs after-school care beginning at 3:00 when school is in session, five days a week for thirty-two weeks a year or 400 hours per year. The parents work all summer, which means that Michael needs care for 25 hours a week for sixteen weeks or 560 hours a year. He's also involved in sports, Sunday school, and music lessons, and he likes to visit friends for a total of 10 additional hours a week, forty-eight weeks a year. Add these hours together, and he needs a minimum of 1,494 hours of care from people other than his parents. If you add in 7 hours of school per day, this adds another 1,120 hours per year, totaling 4,240 hours of care per year, or 44 percent of his waking time. Since it is likely that Mary and Michael will be cared for by different people, their parents oversee 3,120 hours of care provided by a variety of people each year, which is a lot of hours to keep track of on top of everything else parents must do. How on earth can parents monitor every aspect of their children's lives?

There is no way to know for sure if our children will be 100 percent safe with other people, so parents play the odds. The problem with gambling is that on the surface, the odds may look pretty good. Will our children be safe while we are away from them? Facts indicate that abuse, neglect, and maltreatment are most likely to be inflicted upon children by a family member or people who they know well; it is estimated that there is only a one in five thousand chance that a child will be abused by a nonfamily caretaker, such as a child-care worker, teacher, or youth counselor. These odds are similar to the odds of dying in an automobile crash. Should this figure make us worried or relieved?

Children are exposed to different kinds of abuse. Child abuse can consist of active maltreatment—which is direct, intentional, and strategic and includes neglecting, hitting, raping, molesting, calling the child hateful names, or psychologically torturing a child—or it can be passive, indirect, and much harder to define. Passive abuse includes either unintentional maltreatment or behavior that is not readily perceived to be abusive by an outsider but which is actually designed by the perpetrator to deny the child nurturance and care. The age of a child can influence abuse; younger children are more at risk, because they are incapable of getting the help or resources (like food and water) they need for survival, while older children have the verbal and cognitive capabilities to ask for help. Sexual abuse happens to children of all ages and to both boys and girls. Emotional abuse can devastate children of any age but appears to affect younger children the most, as they can understand that people are treating them badly but do not yet have the self-esteem to fight off emotional or verbal assaults.

Knowing what to look for can help parents identify worthy caregivers. Unfortunately, many parents buy into commonly held myths that impede their ability to evaluate caregivers. In order to keep kids safe, it is time to address common myths head-on.

COMMON CAREGIVING MYTHS

Myth 1: Most children do not have care provided by "other people."

Every child is watched over by someone other than its parents at some time, whether at daycare or school or during recreation or social activities. According to the American Bar Association and the U.S. Bureau of the Census, eighty-seven million children eighteen and younger are in the care of people other than their parents at any given point in time. Over 84 percent of four-year-olds receive nonparental care according to the Casey Foundation.

Myth 2: It is possible for parents to find a risk-free caregiver for children.

No situation is totally risk-free. The reality is that accidents sometimes happen, even in the best of circumstances. Most parents assume a certain degree of acceptable risk for their children; they decide whether it safer for their child to attend an after-school program or stay at his friend's house. Parents can reduce the potential for danger if they know what to look for, what questions to ask, and how to advocate for their child.

Myth 3: It is always better for children to be with their parents.

Kids need time away from their parents. Children learn new skills when they are with other people; they achieve successes that are clearly their own, and they develop healthy relationships with others that enable them to become competent and self-sufficient individuals. Children who regularly attend high-quality care or educational programs have been found to be well-adjusted, demonstrate good work habits, develop healthy relationships with peers, possess longer attention spans, acquire better cognitive, language, and reading skills, do better in school, and engage in less antisocial behavior, watch less TV, and display less aggression than other children. Whether learning how to skate, play the piano, hammer a nail, or act in a play, children gain valuable skills from others. Children's participation in recreational, sports, and voluntary organizations provides them with opportunities for personal growth as they build social relationships, learn to cooperate and share, resolve difficulties, and have fun.

Myth 4: People who work with children have been screened and found to be competent.

Organizations are supposed to investigate employees and volunteers, but there is wide variation in this practice. Some employers, such as public schools or the Girl Scouts of America, require thorough background checks. Others, like volunteer organizations or less-formalized daycare centers, may do less-rigorous checks. There are almost 2 million licensed child-care providers, 6.5 million school employees, 15.5 million adults working in youth development and volunteer organizations, 35 million working in health and mental health services, and millions more volunteers who work with children. Most of these people are not heavily screened. Parents should realize that most organizations do not screen employees as thoroughly as they should. Screening often means a criminal background check, and little more.

Myth 5: If a person has a track record of working with kids, they're probably a safe bet.

While experience and credentials may indicate that the provider has the education or training to attend to the needs of children, these are no guarantee. Sometimes pedophiles build up extensive resumes working with children in order to give them access to other kids. For example, Ronald Goff, a retired Illinois principal, was convicted for molesting boys he met while serving as a church camp volunteer and Boy Scout leader.

Myth 6: Strangers are more likely to hurt your child than family or friends.

Data clearly indicates children have a much greater chance of being abducted, abused, or killed by people they know, not by strangers. We teach children about "stranger danger," but most physical and sexual abuse of children is perpetrated by parents, relatives, or friends. Data from the National Center of Child Abduction at the University of New Hampshire indicate that most kidnapped children are snatched by people they know—not by strangers. The fact that the people emotionally closest to your children are actually the ones likeliest to harm them is difficult for most people to accept; hence, the popularity of the "stranger danger" myth.

Myth 7: People who take care of other people's kids do so because they love children.

Some people care for other people's children out of genuine interest and concern, while others do it for financial, professional, civic, or social rewards. People may work with children merely because it's easy to get a job doing it. The uniformly low salaries most child-care workers earn cannot be counted on to motivate good behavior.

Myth 8: As long as kids are safe, what the caregiver does with them isn't that important.

Parents may prefer Grandma's care over that of a trained early childhood professional, but going to the store or watching TV with Granny may not be as stimulating as a well-developed child-oriented preschool curriculum. While keeping children's bodies safe is obviously important, so are the types of educational and emotional experiences children are exposed to while they're with the caregiver. Children need high-quality, appropriate stimulation to help them learn and develop positive self-esteem and behavior patterns.

Myth 9: Caregiving is important for young children but not for teenagers.

Young children need high-quality care, but so do older kids. While adolescents may appear self-sufficient and independent, they still need supervision and guidance. Adolescents spend over 40 percent of their waking time in discretionary settings, usually with other people. As older children get involved with sports, clubs, jobs, and recreational pursuits, they may have more opportunities to be victimized. Unsupervised time is linked with substance abuse, sexual experimentation, and delinquent behavior. Teens need parental guidance and oversight just as much as young children do, only in a different way.

Myth 10: Caregiver abuse hasn't been found to be much of a problem.

There's plenty of evidence to indicate that people should be concerned about children's safety. Studies by the National Association for the Education of Young Children, the American Academy of Pediatrics, the National Commission on Children, the Children's Defense Fund, the Child Welfare League of America, the American Bar Association's Center on Children and the Law, the Carnegie Foundation, Head Start, the FBI, and the Nonprofit Risk Management Center all suggest that children may be at risk when they're in the care of other people.

Myth 11: Most childcare providers are licensed or accredited.

Some states certify that providers meet a particular standard, but which providers and which standards can vary a great deal. In some states only day-care centers are inspected; camps and informally run programs may not be licensed because there are not enough inspectors. Reports indicate that over 80 percent of all family child-care providers are not regulated. Similarly, many coaches are volunteers and have no training about how to work with children.

Myth 12: Parents should be suspicious when their children are with other people.

Most people do an adequate job caring for other people's kids. There are plenty of outstanding programs and exemplary people who provide high-quality care. It would be a shame to deny children those experiences and relationships. If parents are careful and do their homework, they can increase the safety of their children when they are in the care of other people.

Myth 13: You can't trust children's reports about adults, because children tend to complain even when nothing bad has happened.

When children enjoy going somewhere, parents can tell. Happy kids don't make allegations of abuse. Unhappy, scared, or resistant children may complain when they feel unsafe with certain people. Because abuse can take different forms, children may find it difficult to articulate what happened to them, but even very young children give behavioral indicators when they are afraid.

Myth 14: Most of the time when children are hurt, it is because providers are mean.

The most common of all types of child injury comes not from malicious intent, but from negligence or bad judgment. Negligence occurs when normal, reasonable people make mistakes or miscalculations that result in the injury or death of a child.

Myth 15: Parents can rely on trust to make sure their children are safe.

Trust is not enough to ensure children's safety. Parents must investigate which care situations are safe and which aren't. Good-quality care is an investment in your child's future; poor care can do lasting harm. Parents must be vigilant consumers by questioning providers and monitoring care situations to ensure that their children will be safe.

READING THE SAFETY BLUEPRINT

Parents may not be sure how to identify whether a care situation is good for their children, and as a result, they may overreact or underreact. These are inappropriate responses. In order for children to receive quality care, parents need to know what to look for in assessing care situations. Caregivers need to be clear about what they will and will not do. The community has an obligation to make sure there are resources available for children. This triangular relationship between parents, providers, and community is key in creating safety.

Safeguards increase when parents have a contractual arrangement with providers. In contractual care, both parents and caregivers have a clear understanding of what to expect from each other. There may be a monetary exchange in which the parent pays the caregiver for a specific service (i.e. daycare, sports leagues), but a contractual obligation can exist even when no money is involved (i.e. public school, when neighbors agree to babysit your child). In *continuous contractual care,* such as when you contract with the daycare center to take care of your child, providers agree to give certain types of care to the child in exchange for a specific price. It is a business arrangement in which both parent and provider adhere to the contractual agreement, negotiate it, or terminate it if the contract has been violated. *Continuous noncontractual care* is informal. There may be no payment or obligation to provide care in any particular way. An example of this is grandma care. Grandmothers usually don't get paid for watching their grandchildren and want to care for them in their own way, which may be at variance with what the parents prefer. Both contractual and noncontractual care can be effective, but when there is a disagreement over the quality of care, negotiations are more difficult in a relationship that's based on bonds of affection rather than a business contract.

Most of the time parents don't contract with people who have contact with their children; they simply trust the piano teacher, soccer coach, or Cub Scout leader. Parents are reluctant to view such interactions as a form of business exchange, even when money is transferred. Most parents want to believe that people working with kids do so because they like children and find it awkward to ask questions that may display mistrust. But asking questions is a way to make sure that safeguards are in place. The longer the child is going to be in the care of someone, such as 8–5:00, Monday–Friday daycare, the more likely there is to be a contract, especially if the daycare is an official business. The more formalized the organization, such as a summer camp, the more likely it is that a contract may exist. The more intermittent and casual the contact with children, such as when Uncle takes the kids to the park or when a child stays overnight at another friend's house, the less likely there is to be an agreed-upon understanding of what the care entails. When relationships are business transactions, parents may feel justified removing children from the care of people who aren't doing their job well, but parents are less likely to do so with friends and family. These informal caregiving situations are problematic; parents don't know how hard to press to make sure their kids will be safe, because if they push too hard they could destroy the relationship and forfeit the child care. Do contracts make kids safer? Probably. Standards provide parents and caregivers with clear expectations and imply that action could be taken if the agreement is violated. But they can be awkward to implement, especially in emotion-based relationships.

Parents who are aware of potential caregiving risks are likely to survey situations and providers carefully. The factors predicting safe or risky conditions for children in the care of other people are pretty straightforward if parents know what to look for. Researchers have found that certain behaviors are frequently associated with high-risk conditions for children. These are red flags that can alert parents to the potential of danger. Other factors have been identified that tend to protect children from risk and give parents the green light to go ahead with a caregiving situation.

When parents know how to compare protective factors to risk factors, they'll have a better understanding about what the potential risks are. By looking at the interaction of child factors, parent factors, provider factors, and community factors, parents can tell whether a sturdy safety net has been woven to protect their children.

A TOOLKIT FOR KEEPING KIDS SAFE

I have created a toolkit to give parents a set of steps to follow to increase their children's safety when they are with other people. These steps are applicable to a wide variety of care situations.

Step 1: Determine what you need.

Knowing what kind of care you need, the provider characteristics you want, and what you are willing to pay for care all influence your decision about what kind of caregiver to look for. Appropriate care depends upon a child's age, abilities, interests, and needs, but it must also address parents' needs. For instance, Liz and Rich Caluder needed daycare for their two preschoolers. Ruby Booker wanted her son to experience a positive relationship with a male role model. Rhonda Barquist needed a babysitter to pick her daughter up from school, take her to music lessons, and prepare dinner. These parents had to decide exactly what they wanted before they could look for a provider.

Step 2: Identify potential providers.

Once parents know what kind of care they need, the next step is to find the best person to provide it. Before parents decide which babysitter, coach, or camp they'll choose, they have homework to do. Who in the community provides those services? If there are few choices, the decision may be easier, but not necessarily better. If there are several babysitters or camps from which to choose, which are best? Sometimes referral organizations like the American Camp Association can give details about particular types of camps. While referral agencies help parents to narrow the list, they are not always available, leaving parents on their own to search out provider leads.

When parents have multiple options, I advise them to first prioritize which people or programs are best for them, and then try to get their top choice. The caregiver's reputation, cost, location, program content, staff qualifications, and facilities influence which people are most desirable. Liz Caulder found dozens of child-care programs in her city and narrowed her list by selecting those which were on her route to work. She asked other parents if they knew anything about the programs she'd selected, and then she called to see if the recommended ones had openings. She came up with a list of three centers that might be appropriate, and she visited them in order to decide which one to try.

Step 3: Check out the providers.

Investigate! The more information you have about potential providers, the sounder your decision about whether you can trust them. This may require interviews, detailed reference checks, observation of the provider at work, or intuition. It is important to evaluate providers before children are put into their care. This means talking with the staff and looking at the surroundings. Are the children happy and well cared for? Are they doing interesting things? Is the environment safe? Do the people who work there seem competent and attentive? What is their philosophy of children and caregiving? Ask the caregiver to describe the ideal child, as well as impressions of a problematic child. Do you think your child will fit in? If parents like what they see and feel comfortable there, their children probably will too.

While parents may feel uncomfortable interviewing providers, if they don't ask detailed questions about care they won't get details about how the care is provided. Quality providers won't mind questions. Organizations should have conducted background checks on every employee that should be in their personnel files, but they may not be able to share that information with parents. Employees have a right to privacy, just as parents have a right to information. The organization can tell parents general information such as how staff are screened, turnover rates, and other facts that will help them decide if this is a suitable caregiving situation. Usually, when parents contract with individual caregivers, they're on their own to do the background checks. Find out if complaints have ever been filed against the person or agency with the police, licensing organization, Better Business Bureau, or Department of Consumer Affairs. Criminal checks indicate whether the person has past violent, abusive, substance, transportation, financial, or other criminal violations. Parents are advised to identify the criteria used for background checks and not to mistake process for content. Background checks should look at past behavior, but they should also help parents to predict what the caregiver's future behavior will be like. Health assessments or psychological examinations may also be included in background checks. It is important to get references, but parents must ask detailed questions to gain an accurate picture of what kind of care they can expect.

Parents are encouraged to inquire about the *six P's of provider attention,* which include:

Personnel. All caregivers are not equal—not in training and not in the quality of care they provide. They vary significantly in degree of maturity, planning, organization, regulation, flexibility, and responsibility. Parents are advised to ask questions like: What are the qualifications of the people overseeing your child? How are staff screened, hired, trained, supervised, monitored, and evaluated? Do volunteers adhere to the same standards as employees? Is the ratio of children-to-staff low enough to give individual attention? Qualifications, salary, and benefits influence the kind of care children receive. Having many adults available is usually better for children than receiving care provided by one person.

Program and philosophy. Every provider and organization has its own philosophy, program, and activities. Parents need to find one that fits their child's needs. Everyone has a different philosophy about how to interact with children, so it is important for parents to find providers whose philosophy mirrors their own. What is their position on children's autonomy and independence? What is their philosophy toward play? Do parents agree with the provider's disciplinary procedures? The way little things are handled can have a big impact. Knowing the history of the program can be useful in helping parents to identify its philosophy and organizational structure. The goals and objectives of the program should be clearly stated. This will help parents to determine whether a program is a good match for their kids.

Premises. Check the safety of both indoor and outdoor spaces, especially those designated for younger children. How safe are the areas where children engage in routine activities, and how well are they monitored? Some components are visible (handrails on stairs) while others are invisible (pesticides or presence of guns). Indoor facilities should adhere to safety codes and regulations, have clean food preparation areas, easy access, good lighting, safe shower and toilet facilities, reasonable hot water temperature, smoke alarms, emergency exits, and safe sleeping conditions for children. Outdoor facilities should be free from barriers, obstacles, holes, or wildlife that could endanger children. Inspection reports should be available from public health, fire, and state credentialing officials. If providers take the children to offsite locations, such as to the beach or hiking, parents need to know how these environments will be controlled to ensure safety.

Participants. Parents will want to decide if the other children will be positive or negative influences on their own child. Are the ages, behaviors, and personalities of the other participants going to help their child grow and develop, or could they pose physical and emotional problems? How are social relations between participants handled to maximize fun and safety? Is cooperation or competition the norm? Are children left alone in situations where they could get in trouble? The program can look good, but care is always provided in a community context. The strengths and weaknesses of others will influence your child. Environments that embrace tolerance and diversity provide learning opportunities for children; when children feel marginal, scared, bullied, or ridiculed, these environments foster problems.

Prevention. Prevention is always best. Good providers anticipate problems and institute safeguards to avoid them. Child abuse prevention policies should be in place. Parents should know what the provider's attitude toward discipline is and whether corporal punishment, such as spanking or physical restraints, is allowed. Children need to have their privacy protected, especially in toileting, sleeping, and clothes-changing areas. Parents must make clear to providers who can, and cannot, remove the child from their care. For instance, tensions between divorced or separated parents can pose problems for providers, so if one parent is not allowed to visit or leave with a child, staff must know this. A common safety procedure is the use of a sign in/out procedure so the provider knows who is on the premises and when a child is removed. Parents should determine if the facility is clean, whether staff members use appropriate language around children, if toxic substances are present, and if staff is trained to handle emergencies.

Partnership protocols. When parents and providers work together, kids benefit. Smooth interactions don't necessarily come naturally. They result when protocols are in place that delineate clear operating procedures for both parents and caregivers. A handbook of services that contains information about what will be provided, hours of operation, costs, and the responsibilities of parents can reduce chances of miscommunication. When providers are treated like professionals, they tend to give better care. Problems are easier to resolve when there is a partnership already in place.

Step 4: The trial run.

In order to find out if a caregiving situation is as good as it appears, a trial run is essential. The trial run can be as short as a few hours or as long as a few weeks. During that time, the child can communicate whether he is happy there. Parents and providers learn what to expect from each other. A trial period gives people an escape route if the fit isn't right.

Step 5: See it in writing.

Application materials, service handbooks, consent forms, and contracts help clarify what parents can expect from providers. Clearly defined policies and practices prevent potential problems. If no forms are signed and there is only verbal agreement, problems could arise. Save all correspondence, which may be useful later on.

Step 6: Parent participation.

Safe kids are no accident. They need ongoing involvement from their parents. In new situations everyone is usually on good behavior, but over time, as people feel more comfortable with one another, guards are let down. Subsequent care may contradict what was originally promised. Parents should not make assumptions about how things are going. They have to find out. Strategies include:

- Regularly communicating with the children
- Monitoring care received and caregiver interactions
- Discussing care with other parents
- Implementing written procedures
- Identifying unwritten procedures
- Visiting unexpectedly
- Volunteering at events
- Addressing issues as soon as problems occur
- Creating solutions to avoid future difficulties

Step 7: Decide if it is safe.

Safety is not one-dimensional. There are different kinds of risk that parents should minimize. These include:

Environmental safety. How safe is the neighborhood? Are hazardous businesses nearby? Do pollutants on the premises expose the children to harmful substances (such as pesticides, asbestos, or secondhand smoke)? Are there animals nearby that could hurt the children?

Structural safety. How safe is the building that will house the children? Are there loose wires, broken windows, uncovered power outlets, or an insufficient number of fire exits? Do the smoke alarms work? Is the equipment, whether inside the building or outside, safe and age-appropriate? What is the condition of the vehicles in which the child could ride? Where children congregate must be secure and safe.

Physical safety. What disciplinary procedures are used? How are conflicts handled between peers? Is there an open-door policy at the facility, or can anyone just wander in? What are the health and safety standards that are used? Do children have access to guns or weapons? Are they are kept away from poisons? Is sun exposure minimized? Are attempts made to prevent sleep conditions that could lead to Sudden Infant Death Syndrome (SIDS)?

Sexual safety. Since sexual abuse occurs most easily in confined areas where few people have access, is there an open-door policy, and are diapering and toileting areas for young children visible? Adolescents and teens may be confronted with different types of risk, so policies on touching, harassment, and rape are necessary.

Emotional safety. How is the psychological well-being of children protected? What attempts are made to prevent verbal abuse of children?

Violations of privacy. How is private, confidential information about children protected? Do staff members gossip, discuss children or their families with others, or distribute children's phone numbers or addresses?

Step 8: Communicate!

Parents and providers need to communicate effectively with each other. Providers need to know when there are special events or problems at home that may impact the children. Parents need to know about their children's successes and challenges. People have different assumptions about what constitutes good care, so communication is necessary to establish a mutual understanding.

Step 9: Evaluate care.

Parents need regular feedback from children and providers, so it is useful to create regular opportunities to talk about how the care situation is progressing. It could be that both parents and providers have concerns that each feel awkward addressing. Predetermined evaluation times create a vehicle for everyone to work better together. As children grow, their needs change. Family needs shift over time. Providers and organizations may have new demands or opportunities placed before them. As a result, it is appropriate to anticipate opportunities to sit down together and review. Without these opportunities for dialogue, providers cannot know with certainty what is working well or identify areas for improvement.

Step 10: Renew or redo.

After a while it should be clear whether the relationship the child has with a caregiver should continue or be terminated. If the providers are doing well, it's good to reward them; financial increases are always welcome, as are small gifts or letters of support written to their supervisors. If care isn't satisfactory or it isn't improved after discussion, it's time to look for a provider that will better fit the family's needs. Studies indicate that only a quarter of parents believe their children receive high-quality care. If the provider is unsatisfactory to the point of being dangerous, licensing agencies, the Better Business Bureau, professional associations, or the police should be informed. After all, wouldn't you want other parents to do the same for you?

THE RISK-PROTECTION MODEL FOR DETERMINING CHILD-CAREGIVER SAFETY

I have developed a quick and easy method for parents to assess whether a caregiver is appropriate for their child. The Care Assessment Model (CAM) can be used to score key attitudes and behavior of children, parents, and providers. The score can predict how safe the caregiving situation may be for a child. Parents can circle the number that best reflects their experience with a provider; a quick scan will tell them if the caregiving situation is safe or risky. If parents cannot answer a question, this could indicate a risk factor and should be coded as a zero. Too many zeros are a sign to parents that they need to find out more information so their children can be better cared for.

PART A: CHILD BEHAVIOR AND ATTITUDES

High Risk		*Low Risk*
Child seems:		
Scared	0 1 2 3 4 5 6 7 8 9 10	Happy

High Risk		Low Risk
Needy, dependent	0 1 2 3 4 5 6 7 8 9 10	Independent, self-sufficient
Withdrawn	0 1 2 3 4 5 6 7 8 9 10	Assertive
Bored, alienated	0 1 2 3 4 5 6 7 8 9 10	Engaged
Challenged	0 1 2 3 4 5 6 7 8 9 10	Adept
Emotional	0 1 2 3 4 5 6 7 8 9 10	In control
Immature	0 1 2 3 4 5 6 7 8 9 10	Responsible
Isolated	0 1 2 3 4 5 6 7 8 9 10	Social

Child has:		
Poor health	0 1 2 3 4 5 6 7 8 9 10	Good health
Inappropriate communication	0 1 2 3 4 5 6 7 8 9 10	Appropriate communication
No support system	0 1 2 3 4 5 6 7 8 9 10	Extensive support system

Children's behavior and attitudes can vary depending on how comfortable they feel. While children's personalities must be considered, the CAM regards a high score as an indication that children are in a positive environment that puts them at low risk, while a low score is an indication that the children are in a situation where they may not feel safe. A score of 85–110 indicates that the children are engaged and have positive care attitudes, signs that they feel physically and emotionally protected; a score of 44–84 implies some risk, while a score of 11–43 indicates that they are in a high-risk caregiving situation.

PART B: PARENT BEHAVIOR AND ATTITUDES

High Risk		Low Risk
No provider background or reference check	0 1 2 3 4 5 6 7 8 9 10	Extensive background and reference check
Never checked surroundings	0 1 2 3 4 5 6 7 8 9 10	Evaluate internal and external surroundings
Never volunteer	0 1 2 3 4 5 6 7 8 9 10	Active volunteer
Never visit and observe	0 1 2 3 4 5 6 7 8 9 10	Frequent visits and observation

High Risk		*Low Risk*
Never meet with provider	0 1 2 3 4 5 6 7 8 9 10	Ongoing monitoring
Poor communi-cation skills	0 1 2 3 4 5 6 7 8 9 10	Great communication skills
Not confident of care	0 1 2 3 4 5 6 7 8 9 10	Confident care will be good

A score of 56–70 indicates that parents have done a pretty good job trying to prevent caregiver abuse; a score of 28–55 indicates that parents could do a better job finding out more about the caregiver, and a score of 7–28 indicates the parents aren't being as attentive as they need to be.

PART C: PROVIDER BEHAVIOR AND ATTITUDES

High Risk		*Low Risk*
No training	0 1 2 3 4 5 6 7 8 9 10	Extensive training
No experience	0 1 2 3 4 5 6 7 8 9 10	Extensive experience
No application process	0 1 2 3 4 5 6 7 8 9 10	Detailed application process
Not paid	0 1 2 3 4 5 6 7 8 9 10	Well paid with benefits
Haphazard activities	0 1 2 3 4 5 6 7 8 9 10	Well-designed activities
Tense	0 1 2 3 4 5 6 7 8 9 10	Relaxed
Boring	0 1 2 3 4 5 6 7 8 9 10	Fun
No emergency plans	0 1 2 3 4 5 6 7 8 9 10	Emergency plan
Personal problems present	0 1 2 3 4 5 6 7 8 9 10	No physical, emotional, legal, or social problems
Inappropriate facilities	0 1 2 3 4 5 6 7 8 9 10	Appropriate facilities
Abusive punish-ment used	0 1 2 3 4 5 6 7 8 9 10	Nonviolent, instructive discipline
Unsafe transportation	0 1 2 3 4 5 6 7 8 9 10	Safe transportation
Prior problems	0 1 2 3 4 5 6 7 8 9 10	Good history

High Risk		Low Risk
References unavailable or unwilling to talk	0 1 2 3 4 5 6 7 8 9 10	References provide feedback

A score of 110–140 indicates that providers are probably a safe bet; a score of 109–139 means that the provider does not have the program attributes needed to ensure safe and satisfied clients, while a scores under 109 indicates that there is a high degree of risk.

Common Red Flags

Knowing where problems lie ahead of time is crucial. Some commonly found red flags include:

- Poor enrollment process
- Reluctance to give names of others who have used the provider
- No drop-in policy
- Small number of qualified staff
- Caregivers without significant age-appropriate relationships
- Caregivers who have health problems, low self-esteem, criminal records, or use substances
- Inadequate facilities
- No license or credentials
- Inability to provide regular, detailed communication and information
- Insufficient monitoring, assessment procedures, and evaluation
- Presence of unauthorized adults
- "Trust me" emphasis

SUMMARY

Making a good decision about what caregiver to choose isn't a one-step procedure. It takes a lot of work, diligence, and ongoing attentiveness. Parents—even educated, well-meaning ones—may not know how to distinguish safe care situations from risky ones. Being a good parent is not something that you inherently are—it is something that you learn to become. Getting good at it takes a tremendous amount of time, energy, networking, monitoring, and observation. Let us now look at specific types of caregiving situations so that parents can learn what to look for in order to better protect their children.

Afterschool Alliance
1616 H St., NW
Washington, DC 20006
(202) 347-1002
http://www.afterschoolalliance.org

American Academy of Pediatrics
141 Northwest Point Blvd.
Elk Grove Village, IL, 60007
(847) 434-4000
http://www.aap.org

American Bar Association Center on
Children and the Law
321 North Clark Street
Chicago, IL 60610
(312) 988-5000
http://www.abanet.org

Carnegie Foundation
437 Madison Avenue
New York, NY 10022
(212) 371-3200
http://www.carnegie.org

Children's Defense Fund
25 E Street, NW
Washington, DC 20001
(202) 628-8787
(800) CDF-1200 (800-233-1200)
http://www.childrensdefense.org

Child Welfare League of America
440 First Street, NW, Third Floor
Washington, DC 20001-2085
(202) 638-2952
http://www.cwla.org

Head Start
Administration for Children and
Families
370 L'Enfant Promenade, SW
Washington, DC 20201
(617) 565-1020
http://www2.acf.dhhs.gov/programs/
hsb

National Association for the Education of
Young Children
1509 16th St., NW
Washington, DC 20036
(202) 232-8777
(800) 424-2460
http://www.naeyc.org

National Center for Missing and
Exploited Children
699 Prince St.
Alexandria, VA 22314
1-800-THE-LOST (800-843-5678)
www.cybertipline.com

Nonprofit Risk Management Center
1130 Seventeenth Street, NW, Suite 210
Washington, DC 20036
(202) 785-3891
http://www.nonprofitriskmanagement
.com

United States Government
After School Programs
http://www.afterschool.gov

Adams, Gina. *Massachusetts: Child Care Challenges*. Washington, D.C.: Children's Defense Fund, May 1998.

Adams, Gina, and Nicole Oxendine Poersch. *Key Facts About Child Care and Early Education: A Briefing Book*. Washington, D.C.: Children's Defense Fund, 1997.

Annie E. Casey Foundation. *Child Care You Can Count On: Programs and Policies*. Baltimore, Md. 1999.

Arnette, J. L. "Hiring the Right People." *School Safety* (Spring 1994): 4–8.

Barasch, Douglas. "Would You Hurt this Baby? How a New Wave of Apathy Puts All Children at Risk." *Redbook* (1998): 124–130.

Bevill, Alica, and David Gast. "Social Safety for Young Children: A Review of the Literature on Safety Skills Instruction." *Topics in Early Childhood Special Education* 18, no. 4 (Winter, 1998): 222–238.

Carnegie Foundation. *"Mobilize Communities to Support Young Children and their Families."* 1999. http://www.carnegie.org/ starting_points/startp5.html.

———. *"Starting Points: Meeting the Needs of Our Youngest Children."* 1994. http://www.carnegie.org.

Casper, Lynne. "Who's Minding Our Preschoolers?" *Current Population Reports*. United States Bureau of the Census. Washington, D.C.: Government Printing Office, 1997.

Child Care Action Campaign. *Dealing with Sexual Abuse: A Guide for Parents*, 22. New York, N.Y., 2002.

Children's Defense Fund. *The State of America's Children*. Washington, D.C.: Children's Defense Fund, 2005.

Children's Foundation. *Family Child Care Licensing Study*. Washington, D.C.: The Children's Foundation, 1999.

Child Welfare League of America. *Standards of Excellence for Services for Abused or Neglected Children and Their Families*. Washington, D.C., 1998.

Costin, Lela, Howard Karger, and David Stoesz. *The Politics of Child Abuse in America*. New York: Oxford University Press, 1996.

Daly, Daniel, and Thomas Dowd. "Characteristics of Effective, Harm-free Environment for Children in Out of Home Care." *Child Welfare* 71, no. 6 (December 1992): 486–496.

Daro, Deborah, and Cing-Tung Wang. *Current Trends in Child Abuse Reporting and Fatalities*. Chicago: National Committee to Prevent Child Abuse, 1997.

Farmer, Tom, and Laurel Sweet. "Reardon Faces 122 Counts of Child Abuse Indictment." *Boston Herald*. 1 August 2000, A1.

Fiene, Richard. *"13 Indicators of Quality Childcare."* National Resource Center for Health and Safety in Child Care. University of Colorado. 2002. http:// aspe.hhs.gov/hsp/ccquality-ind02.

Fight Crime. *"America's Front Line Against Crime: A School and Youth Violence Prevention Plan."* 2006. http://www.fightcrime.org/reports/schoolviol.htm.

Finkelhor, David. *A Sourcebook on Child Sexual Abuse*. Thousand Oaks, Calif.: Sage, 1986.

Finkelhor, David, Gerald Hotaling, and Andrea Sedlak. "Missing, Abducted, Runaway, and Throwaway Children in America." Washington, D.C.: Government Printing Office, 1990.

Fortin, Andree, and Claire Chamberland. "Preventing the Psychological Maltreatment of Children." *Journal of Interpersonal Violence* 3 (10 September 1995): 275–296.

Galinsky, Ellen. *The Costs of NOT Providing Quality Early Childhood Programs*. Washington, D.C.: National Association for the Education of Young Children, 2000.

Gardner, Marilyn. "A+ Caregivers." *Working Mother* (July 1995): 26–28.

Giardino, Angelo P., and Eileen R. Giardino. "Recognition of Child Abuse." *American Academy of Pediatrics*. Chicago: Elsevier, 2002.

Goodmark, Leigh. *Keeping Kids Out of the System: Creative Legal Practice As a Community Child Protection Strategy*. Chicago: American Bar Association, Center on Children and the Law, 2000.

Gough, B., and P. Reavey. "Parental Accounts Regarding the Physical Punishment of Children: Discourses of Disempowerment." *Child Abuse and Neglect* 21, no. 5. (May 1997): 417–430.

Grubb, W. N., and Marvin Lazerson. *Broken Promises: How Americans Fail Their Children*. Chicago: University of Chicago Press, 1988.

Hart, Jordana. "Statistics Say Abuse Hits Close to Home: Most Young Victims Know Their Molester." *Boston Globe*, 30 May 2000, B1.

Hopper, Jim. *Child Abuse: Statistics, Research and Resources*. 2005. http://www.jimhopper.com/abstats.

Jackson, Shelly, Ross Thompson, Elaine Christiansen, Rebecca Colman, Jennifer Wyatt, Chad Buckendahl, Brian Wilcox, and Reece Peterson. "Predicting Abuse Prone Parental Attitudes and Discipline Practices in a Nationally Representative Sample." *Child Abuse and Neglect* 23, no. 1 (1999): 15–29.

Jacobs, Francine, and Margery Davies, eds. *More than Kissing Babies?: Current Child and Family Policy in the United States*. Westport, Conn.: Auburn House, 1999.

Kendrick, Ally Shapiro, Roxanne Kaufmann, and Katherine Messenger. *Healthy Young Children: A Manual for Programs*. Washington, D.C.: National Association for the Education of Young Children, 1995.

———. *Healthy Young Children: A Manual for Programs*. Washington, D.C.: National Association for the Education of Young Children, 2000.

Killam, Edward. "A Guide to Child Care Services." *FBI Law Enforcement Bulletin* (June 1995): 21–25.

Knudsen, Dean. *Child Maltreatment: Emerging Perspectives.* New York: General Hall, 2005.

Koralek, Derry. *Caregivers of Young Children: Preventing and Responding to Child Maltreatment.* National Center on Child Abuse and Neglect. U.S. Department of Health and Human Services, Administration for Children and Families. Washington, D.C.: Government Printing Office, 2000.

Lavin, Christine. *Sesame Street Research Report: Childcare from A to Z.* http://www.sesameworkshop.org/parents/advice/article.php?contentId=91964.

Louis Harris and Associates. *Childcare Safety.* Rochester, N.Y., 2005. http://www.harrisinteractive.com.

National Commission on Children. *Beyond Rhetoric: A New American Agenda for Children and Their Families.* Washington, D.C.: National Commission on Children, 1993.

Patterson, John. *Child Abuse Prevention Primer for Your Organization.* Washington, D.C.: Nonprofit Risk Management Center, 2002.

———. *Staff Screening Tool Kit.* Washington, D.C.: Nonprofit Risk Management Center, 2004.

Runyan, Carol, Diana Gray, Jonathon Kotch, and Matthew Kreuter. "Analysis of U.S. Child Care Safety Regulations." *American Journal of Public Health* 81, no. 8 (1991): 981–985.

Schaefer, Charles. "Defining Verbal Abuse of Children." *Psychological Reports* 80, no. 2 (April 1997): 626.

Seidman, Anna, and John Patterson. *Kidding Around? Be Serious! A Commitment to Safe Service Opportunities for Young People.* Washington, D.C.: Nonprofit Risk Center, 1996.

Shore, Rima. *What Kids Need.* Carnegie Foundation. Boston: Beacon Press, 1994.

Shpancer, Noam. "The Gap: Parental Knowledge About Daycare." *Early Child Development & Care* 172, no. 6 (2002): 635–642.

Spencer, J. William, and Dean Knudsen. "Out of Home Maltreatment: An Analysis of Risk in Various Settings for Children." *Children and Youth Services Review* 14 (1992): 485–492.

The Telegraph. "Sentencing of Former Edwardsville Junior High School Principal Ronald Goff." 2005. http://www.zwire.com/site/news.cfm?newsid=466131&BRD=1719&PAG=461&dept_id=25271.

Vachss, Andrew. "Are We Doing Enough to Protect Our Children?" *Parade Magazine,* 2 May 1999.

Vissing, Yvonne, and Walter Baily. "Parent-to-Child Verbal Aggression." In *Communication and Family Violence,* ed. Dudly Cahn and Sally Lloyd. Thousand Oaks, Calif.: Sage Publications, 1996: 127–154.

Warner, Susan. "Caring For Our Children." *University of New Hampshire Magazine* (Winter 1999): 14–16.

Wells, Susan, Noy Davis, Kim Dennis, Rob Chipman, Claire Sandt, and Marsha Liss. *Effective Screening of Childcare and Youth Service Workers.* Washington, D.C.: American Bar Association, Center on Children and the Law, 1999.

Chapter 2 How Safe Is Day Care?

Like other working parents, I relied upon daycare when my children were young. Initially I wanted my children in family-based care, because I thought the children would get more attention in a family-like environment. But many providers had unpredictable hours, and I found myself without scheduled care when they had more pressing things to do. Some cared for too many children and mine had to vie for attention or watch too much television in houses that were sometimes dirty and not kid-proofed. Some providers were inattentive, a few were mean, and some spanked my children even though I made it clear I didn't want them to be physically disciplined. After some mini-crises, I decided to try the only daycare center in town, a church-run one that had lots of toys, sleeping cots, and a clean kitchen. The director had some professional training. Most employees were members of the church. I felt uncomfortable when one young male employee rubbed the children's backs under their shirts during naptime, but female staff did the same thing so I chose to dismiss my concerns. One day when I pulled into the parking lot, my three-year-old son became hysterical and refused to go in because he was "afraid of the man with the dead frog in his pocket." This incident occurred around the same time as national reports aired about daycare centers where staff allegedly hurt animals to frighten children from telling parents that they were being sexually abused. I told the director about my son's fearful response. Her response was one of shock and denial, but she agreed to investigate what had happened. A few days later she came to my home and demanded I sign a legal document that said my son had lied. I refused to sign. While I had no "proof" that the young man showed a dead frog to the children, she had provided no proof that he didn't. Even though my son was young, I trusted him. Why was the director angry and threatening? Something was wrong. I recalled the work of my former child abuse professor, forensic scientist David Walters, who alleged that any time a child is afraid of a caregiver it is an indication of a potential problem. Dr. Walters taught me that happy children don't make complaints of maltreatment. The director's reaction to my inquiry made me concerned that she was more interested in protecting her business than protecting my child.

In comparison, a decade later in a different state, my six-week-old daughter became enrolled in the University of New Hampshire's daycare center where she received excellent care. The center was designed so that bathrooms and sleep areas were constantly monitored. No adult was ever alone with a child, thereby reducing the opportunities for possible abuse. The staff received intense training and ongoing supervision to assure they used the best techniques. Each day parents were given feedback from staff on both positive developments and challenges the child had experienced. I left my daughter there with absolute confidence, knowing that her physical, social, and emotional needs would be safeguarded. While I prided myself on being a good parent, she learned more there than I could have taught her if I had kept her at home. She learned to speak Japanese and visited with dinosaur archeologists from Kenya. She learned to read and entered school fully prepared to seize any academic challenge that confronted her. She made friends, and her self-esteem was high.

When people lived in close-knit communities, they knew everyone else in town, either directly or indirectly. It was possible to get an idea about the kind of care your children would receive before asking another person to watch over them. Before two incomes were required for families to survive, most families had a relative or friend who stayed home and could watch their kids, and care was needed for fewer hours. Today, most parents live without family nearby. They don't always know their neighbors well. They may never even see the person who will be in charge of their children's care until the day they drop them off. They have simply trusted that people who watch other people's kids will do a good job doing so. While some parents are oblivious to danger signs, others put their lives on hold, forgo careers, social, recreational, or civic activities so they can keep their children safe, with them, at home. In either extreme—the parents who trust too much or those who trust too little—the child pays the penalty.

Good care during the early years of life, when physical, cognitive, social, and emotional foundations are being developed, is essential for children. Birth to age three is a critical time in brain development. Environments that are intellectually stimulating and emotionally satisfying help children to become motivated learners and workers. Evidence indicates that quality professional care increases children's self-conception, problem-solving capability, attention span, language acquisition, sociability and social interactions, motor skill development, and cognitive abilities. Researchers found that children in high-quality programs make around $143,000 more over their lifetimes than those who did not get high-quality child care. Because a child's development hinges on the interplay between nature and nurture, early care has long-lasting effects on how kids develop, learn, and regulate their emotions.

Child care quality affects adults as well. When our children receive inadequate care, we are more likely to be late for work, absent, or distracted on the job than parents who have good child care according to the Economic Opportunity Institute in Seattle. Employee absenteeism caused by poor child care costs American business more than $3 billion a year. Mothers of children in high-quality healthcare can also expect greater earnings: about $133,000 more over their lifetime. School districts can expect to save more than $11,000 per child on children enrolled in high-quality child care because they are less likely to require special or remedial education. For every dollar spent on high-quality early education programs, taxpayers can expect four dollars in benefits, according research by the Frank Porter Graham Child Development Institute at the University of North Carolina at Chapel Hill.

The pay-off will be greater in other ways, such as in decreased crime and improved children's health. Yet the United States has not developed a comprehensive system to ensure that all children have high-quality early education or care. There is no national child care system, no financial assistance for most parents, no national training, credentialing, or monitoring mechanisms for providers. Child care is more likely to be regarded as babysitting than education. While excellent child care may be available, the National Association for the Education of Young Children found that 70 percent of parents with young children found good, affordable care extremely difficult to find. Lucky parents can afford quality care, and those who can't are left scrambling to find the best care we can.

Still, out-of-home care is a universal experience for children. There are many kinds of environments from which to choose, and they differ dramatically in form, substance, and quality.

TYPES OF DAYCARE

Daycare centers.

Daycare centers are professionally run programs designed to provide care and education to young children. The first publicly funded center in the

United States opened in 1815, and it was designed to care for infants and very young children, since those over seven went to work (child labor laws didn't exist until the 1900s, and children as young as three commonly did piecework, such as sorting feathers or tobacco). During World War II, when men were away at war and women entered the workforce in droves, many childcare facilities opened, such as Kaiser shipyard's model program in Portland, Oregon. But most closed within two years of the war's end; when the men returned home, women were expected to quit their jobs to become homemakers. Despite the educational and social benefits of daycare, the purpose of daycare has always been to liberate parents so they can work.

Daycare can be provided in private, for-profit, or nonprofit centers. Programs associated with teacher training programs, such as those affiliated with colleges, usually have superior child care programs since they are designed to teach students state-of-the-art skills. Religious-based care programs emphasize a particular ideology, which is fine if parents want their child exposed to that view but problematic if they do not. Some daycare centers are run independently, while others are part of a national or regional chain, such as KinderCare.

The philosophical differences between independent centers and daycare chains can be considerable. Independent centers tend to be unique, with individualized programming that reflects the interests of the providers. Chains provide a more homogenized "everyone does the same thing everywhere on the same day" approach.

There are many benefits to center-based care. A good daycare center should address 100 percent of children's needs 100 percent of the time. They have designated hours that parents can count on, unlike babysitters who may decide at the spur of the moment not to show up. Centers typically have child-size tables, chairs, toilets, and sinks, which are better for both safety and competence-building. There are many children to play with, and there are usually multiple people available to provide care. Research indicates that children who attend high-quality centers are more social, better educated, less aggressive, and better adjusted than children who have not attended quality daycare.

Some daycare centers will not accept children under age two; many require that children be potty-trained. As a result, finding care for infants can be challenging and expensive. Another drawback of daycare centers is that because they have fixed hours of operation, if parents need to drop children off early, pick them up late, or work overnight or weekend hours, care may not be available; if it is, there may be financial penalties for the extended time. This makes reasonable business sense for employees but it is difficult for parents with unpredictable schedules. Another issue is that centers do not want to take sick children, since contagious kids infect other children and adults. Children who are sick may be better off at home, but a no-sick policy can be inconvenient for parents who must get to work. Centers with higher staff-child ratios and less staff training are often more affordable but may find it difficult to help children with special needs. High provider-child ratios put children in a situation where they have to struggle for attention and force workers to change in an environment where the emphasis is on group management. The benefits of a good daycare center can be significant, but bureaucratic and financial considerations can pose difficulties for parents who have extenuating circumstances.

Child care co-ops.

Co-operative centers appeal to many parents who want childcare that cuts costs and encourages greater parent involvement. Parents volunteer to assume both administrative and teaching responsibilities, and they exchange child care with one another at an organized facility on a specified schedule. Co-ops vary in structure and format, but most have an educational curriculum and daily schedule. They tend to be less regulated than formal daycare centers; while a director may be hired, the board of directors and everyday staff consist of parent volunteers. Because of extensive parental involvement, many parents seem to be happy with the kind of care their children receive. A key benefit of this kind of care is that families work together as a community on behalf of the children served. Potential problems are that not all parents have time to donate and some who volunteer do not have good skills or interaction styles. Confronting parent volunteers who do not perform satisfactorily can create a delicate situation, since the essence of a cooperative environment requires that people work together and decide issues pertaining to care and program operations. An inherent tension in child-care co-ops is that some focus less on what children need than on what parents want.

Family-run daycare facilities.

Some parents want the consistency of daycare but do not have the time to volunteer at co-ops. They may prefer family care because there are fewer children and are less formal than daycare centers. The most common arrangement consists of a woman caring for several children in her home. Some states require home daycare centers to be licensed, but many do not. Often parents opt to hire someone they know to watch their children without checking to see if they are licensed or trained in child care. The format, hours, program, policies, and cost of home daycare vary dramatically. In typical family child care, a woman cares for up to six children in her home. There may be assistants if more than six children are present. There should be no more than three infants, four toddlers, or eight children for every one adult. Family daycare is less expensive and has more flexible hours than a formal daycare center. However, home-based care is not necessarily safer than daycare center–provided care. According to the Family Child Care Licensing Study by the Children's Foundation, most (90 percent) family care providers are not regulated and have no contact with regulatory or supportive agencies. Studies have found that half of unregulated family daycare homes give substandard care. Investigators are seldom available to prove that even registered and certified child-care homes meet state standards.

HOW TO CHOOSE A DAYCARE CENTER

Once parents know what to look for in a daycare center, it becomes much easier to find a facility that's right for their family. The first question that parents should ask themselves is:

What do you need and want?

The most basic question to consider is what kind of care is needed. Some parents need care for several children ten hours a day, so they will have different needs than parents who want care for one child while they work part-time or go out to lunch with friends. Some parents may want their children to be exposed to care so they can receive social and educational experiences while others may want their children to play in a less-structured, home-like setting. Once they know what they want, then they can proceed to more detailed questions.

How much can you pay?

Parents must determine how much they can pay for care. Good care can be expensive and cost as much as monthly rent, utility, or grocery payments. Studies by the Annie E. Casey Foundation and Children's Defense Fund found that the average cost of care exceeds $3,000 a year and may be as much as $12,000, which is comparable to college tuition. However, most child-care providers in the United States earn an average of $6.89 per hour, or $12,058 per year, based on thirty-five hours per week for fifty weeks per year—which is less than the average parking lot attendant or carwash employee makes. Some better-paid child-care providers average as much as $15,430 in annual income according to the U.S. Department of Labor, but funeral attendants, bus drivers, garbage collectors, toll-takers, and counter-help at McDonalds usually make more. The national average starting wage for daycare teachers has risen only one cent in eight years. Most child-care providers receive no benefits, health insurance, retirement, vacation time, sick days, or paid leave. Still, because there is no national daycare support program, like Social Security for the elderly, the burden is on parents to pay the high cost of child care. Some resort to lesser-quality care in order to save money, but children usually fare much better with professionally trained teachers.

Is good care accessible?

There are more children who need care than there are providers, and this is especially true for infants. High-quality programs may be expensive and have long waiting lists. Many parents find that between what is available and what they can afford, they don't have many child care choices.

How competent are the providers?

Parents are advised to look closely at the skills, training, expertise, maturity, and judgment of providers. Despite overwhelming evidence that better training means better care for kids, the any-warm-body-will-do attitude remains evident in most people's minds, especially when they find themselves with few choices. Many people's attitude seems to be that since anyone can have a child, anyone can take care of one. The National Child Care Staffing Study confirmed that when neglect and abuse occurs, it is almost always result of inadequately trained and monitored staff. Inadequate training can lead to abuse, as was the case at the Hudson, Massachusetts, A Place To Grow daycare center, where staff put blankets over heads of children to get them to go to sleep, sprayed crying children with water, failed to administer prescribed medications, and duct-taped an eight-month-old infant to a wall of the facility because they thought it was amusing. The national staffing study ranked standards for staff training as unacceptable in almost all fifty states.

Forty states do not require that providers have *any* early-childhood training prior to serving children. Ironically, even hairdressers and manicurists are required by law to have 1,500 hours of training at an accredited school before they can obtain a license. Only nine states meet the minimum recommended teacher training standards for infants—who are the most vulnerable and thus in need of the most highly trained providers—thirty-nine states do not require a single hour of training for home-based providers, and thirty-two states do not demand any prior training for child-care employees.

Are they licensed, accredited, or regulated?

Quality of both family- and center-based care is higher in states with strong child-care regulations, and providers who are licensed and accredited tend to be better caregivers than those who are not. Professional early childhood educators are more likely to join organizations such as the Association for Childhood Education International and the National Association for the Education of Young Children (NAEYC), which have developed standards that encourage optimum care for kids. States may license individuals as providers and license and monitor facilities, but few providers actually get licensed, and most child-care centers fail to meet the higher standards of accreditation. State standards require that children must be immunized, that providers have first aid and CPR training, and that providers wash their hands before and after diapering or when preparing food. While state governments set guidelines and are supposed to enforce requirements, there is wide variation among states, with some like New York imposing stringent standards and states like Texas having fewer ones. Parents may not realize that 40 percent of child-care and education programs—including family child care, church-based programs, and after-school programs—are legally exempt from state regulations. When it comes to adhering to professional standards, NAEYC found that nationally only 6 percent of all child-care settings were accredited and most did not meet the standards established by the American Public Health Association or the American Academy of Pediatrics; only four of the fifty states met the recommended child-staff ratio for infants (California, Kansas, Maryland, and Massachusetts), and only 10 percent of infant classrooms and 34 percent of three-year-olds' classrooms met their standards. The Child Care Bureau found that providers who run informal programs aren't usually licensed and that half of unregulated care providers provide inadequate care. While licensure does not ensure that children will be safe, there is at least some measure of control, whereas unlicensed facilities have no external control. Even those that are licensed are seldom monitored by any external agency, which puts the burden of responsibility on parents. The Annie E. Casey Foundation reports that 90 percent of family child-care providers are not regulated and have no contact with oversight agencies. Many centers avoid being licensed, such as those that operate part-time or those on a drop-in basis such as in shopping malls or exercise clubs. More than half the states don't inspect licensed homes and many fail to track those whose licenses were denied to make sure they're not still caring for kids. Parents are advised to know how tightly regulated the centers are, because regulations are designed to protect their children.

Visit.

Are you welcome to visit anytime? Good centers have an open-door policy for parents to come and go at will, and they welcome parent participation and feedback. It is a bad sign if parents can't drop in anytime. Centers that systematically monitor, supervise, and evaluate the lives of staff and children at the center can reassure parents that risk factors are reduced.

Walk into a center and observe how it feels and what is going on. Does the center feel like a safe, enjoyable place for kids to be? Is the building attractive and clean, especially the food preparation, sleep, and toileting areas? Are there enough teachers around to give children the care and instruction they need? Parents must ask themselves if it is a place where they would feel comfortable leaving their children.

Are the children happy and engaged in activities?

Do they play with age-appropriate toys and activities? Are children doing interesting things that help them to learn? Do they work well with each other and have friends? How many children are angry, crying, sick, or isolated? Do kids ask for adult help easily? Are they trusting or scared? Watching children's behaviors and interactions can tell you a lot about what goes on at the center. If the kids spend much of their time watching television, it's probably not a stimulating place.

Do you like the way the providers interact with and discipline the children?

Are the providers warm, concerned, and caring? Are they authoritarian or flexible? How do you feel about the amount of physical contact providers have with the children? Some parents like their children to be held and hugged, while others feel providers should not be kissing kids or invading children's personal space. Every parent and provider has their own preference about how young children should be disciplined. Do you agree with each other's disciplinary philosophy and practices? In general, if adults use physical force, it's a bad sign. Most discipline, however, isn't physical but verbal and emotional; observe the language providers use around children and whether they are respectful to the children. Watch how children treat other children. Remember, children learn to treat others the way they are treated.

Do the providers seem happy?

Happy staff members get paid well and aren't overworked. Satisfied staff members are treated as professionals by their fellow staff members and by parents. High staff morale means it is a good place to work, which increases safety for kids. If there is a high staff turnover rate, this is a bad sign because it implies that staff members aren't paid adequately or treated professionally. Often staff replacements in high-turnover organizations have poorer credentials and less experience and training than children deserve.

Ask questions.

Visiting the daycare center with your child will give parents lots of information about the center, the staff, and how comfortable your child would be there. Questions to ask daycare providers include:

- What type of training and education do caregivers have?
- How many staff members have left in the past three years?
- What is the teacher-child ratio?
- How long has the center been operating?
- How long has the prospective caregiver been working both there and in child care?
- What is the training and certification level of the staff?
- Is the center licensed? If so, by who? Ask to see the license to make sure it is up to date.
- What is the daily program for children?
- What are meal and nap time procedures?
- How does the caregiver describe ideal and problematic children?
- What is the procedure for parents and staff to use to communicate about the child?

- How are sick children managed?
- Is there a waiting list? If so, this is a good sign that indicates other parents want their children to be there.

Check references of potential providers.

Daycare centers should have background check information on file. If they do not, this could be a sign of trouble. If parents are concerned, they can conduct their own background checks. Always get several opinions.

Follow-up.

Once a center or provider is selected, parents should follow up to determine how well staff are supervised and monitored. It is helpful to meet together and evaluate successes and challenges and to work together collaboratively on behalf of the child. Ongoing monitoring, review, and evaluation are essential parts of the caregiving process. Providers need to earn the parent's trust. Sometimes an oversight organization exists, but if not, parents must do it themselves.

The list of things parents can look for is endless, and parents may have special concerns for addressing the unique needs of their child. But if they are happy with the answers providers give to these basic questions and concerns, it is a good starting place. If they are not satisfied with what they see, the best advice is to keep looking. It may take time to find the right provider, but the search is worth it.

PROMISING PROGRAMS

The Department of Defense (DOD) has the largest child-care system in the nation. It provided less-than-adequate care until the 1980s, when it was hit with a wave of child abuse scandals. Congress established the Military Child Care Act to enforce organizational changes. The DOD's child-care programs had been underfunded with no standards, certifications, or enforced regulations, but the multibillion dollar act promoted quality care that increased the cognitive, social, emotional, and physical development of children at affordable prices. The result was the transformation of the DOD's program into a national model. Staff training hours are twice the national average, teachers receive higher than average pay, classrooms have low adult-child ratios, and strict enforcement of standards, frequent inspections, and regular evaluations are used to document areas of success and need. Active parent involvement and government-subsidized costs have helped to transform a mediocre system of care into one of the nation's best. Over 70 percent of the DOD centers have been accredited by NAEYC compared to fewer than 10 percent of centers nationwide. This model could be realized nationwide, but the government would have to be willing make child care a priority and allocate serious money for it.

RESOURCES

American Academy of Family Physicians
"Day Care: Choosing a Good Center"
http://familydoctor.org/030.xml

Child Care Action Campaign
330 Seventh Ave., 17th Floor
New York, NY 10001
(212) 239-0138

Child Care Aware
2116 Campus Dr., SE
Rochester, MN 55904
(800) 424-2246

Child Care Law Center
221 Pine St., 3rd Floor
San Francisco, CA 94104
(415) 394-7144

Daycare: A Resource for Parents and
Providers
http://www.daycare.com

Day Care Resource Connection
600 Washington St., Suite 6100
Boston, MA 0211
(617) 988-6600
http://www.daycareresource.com

Department of Defense Office of Family
Policy
4015 Wilson Blvd.
Arlington, VA 22202
(703) 696-5733

Ecumenical Child Care Network
8765 W. Higgins Rd., Suite 405
Chicago, IL 60631
(773) 693-4040

Families and Work Institute
267 Fifth Ave., Floor 2
New York, NY 10016
(212) 465-2044
http://www.familiesandwork.org

National Association for the Education of
Young Children
1509 16th St., NW
Washington, DC 20036
(202) 232-8777
http://www.naeyc.org

National Association of Child Care
Resource and Referral Agencies
1319 F Street, NW, Suite 500
Washington, DC 20004
http://NACCRRA.org

National Child Care Association
1016 Rosser St.
Conyers, GA 30207
(800) 543-7161
http://www.nccanet.org

National Child Care Information Center
243 Church St., NW, 2nd Floor
Vienna, VA 22180

National Network for Child Care
University of Iowa
Iowa City, IA 52242
(319) 335-3500
http://www.nncc.org

National Parent Information Network
ERIC Clearinghouse on Elementary and
Early Childhood Education
Children's Research Center
51 Gergty Drive
Campaign, IL 61820
(800) 583-4135

National Resource Center for Health and
Safety in Child Care
University of Colorado Health Sciences
Center
School of Nursing
4200 E. Ninth St., Box C287
Denver, CO 80262
(303) 315-5592

National Safe Kids Campaign
1301 Pennsylvania Ave., NW, Suite 1000
Washington, DC 20004-1707
(202) 662-0600
http://www.safekids.org

Zero to Three: National Center for
Infants, Toddlers and Families
734 15th St., NW, Suite 1000
Washington, DC 20005-2101
(202) 638-1144

REFERENCES

Adams, Gina. *How Safe? The Status of State Efforts to Protect Children in Childcare.* Washington, D.C.: Children's Defense Fund, 1998.

Adams, Gina, and Nicole Oxendine Poersch. *Key Facts About Child Care and Early Education: A Briefing Book.* Washington, D.C.: Children's Defense Fund, 1997.

Adams, Gina, Karen Schulman, and Nancy Ebb. *Locked Doors: States Struggling to Meet the Child Care Needs of Low Income Working Families.* Washington, D.C.: Children's Defense Fund, 1998.

American Journal of Public Health. "Child Outcomes When Childcare Center Classes Meet Recommended Standards for Quality." *American Journal of Public Health* 89, no. 7 (July 1999): 1072–1078.

Annie E. Casey Foundation. *Making Quality Child Care a Reality for America's Low Income Working*

Families. Baltimore, Md.: Kids Count, 1998.

BabyCenter. "Home Daycare: Advantages and Disadvantages." http://www.babycenter.com/refcap/baby/babychildcare/6039.html.

Beach, Betty. "Perspectives on Rural Child Care." *ERIC Digest*. http://www.ericdigests.org/1997-3/rural.html.

Bernstein, Robert. "Who's Minding the Kids?" *Bureau of Census Statistics Brief*. U.S. Department of Commerce. Economics and Statistics Administration. Bureau of the Census. Washington, D.C.: Government Printing Office, 2000.

Blau, David. *The Economics of Child Care*. New York: Russell Sage Foundation, 1991.

Bombardieri, Marcella. "Child Attacked by Pit Bull at Day Care House." *Boston Globe*, 20 June 2000, B1.

Boston Globe. "Middleton Abuse Case Expands Dramatically." 17 June 2000, A1.

———. "Parents Face Higher Tuition Costs for Quality Child Care than for Public College." 29 May 1998.

Bredekamp, Sue, and Barbara A. Willer. eds. *NAEYC Accreditation*. Washington, D.C.: NAEYC, 1997.

Bybee, Deborah, and Carol Mowbray. "Community Response to Child Sexual Abuse in Day Care Settings." *Families in Society* 74 (March 1993): 268–281.

Carnegie Corporation of New York. *Years of Promise: A Comprehensive Learning Strategy for America's Children*. New York: Carnegie Corporation, 1996.

Child Care Aware. "New Research on Brain Development is Important for Parents." http://www.childcareaware.org/en/dailyparent/0397.

Child Care Bureau. *"A Profile of the Child Care Work Force."* http://www.acf.dhhs.gov/ccb/faq/workforc.htm.

Children's Foundation. *1999 Family Child Care Licensing Study*. Washington, D.C.: The Children's Foundation, 1999.

Cole, Caroline Louise. "Hudson Day Care Appealing Suspension." *Boston Globe*, 25 March 2000, B3.

Connor, Lee Lusardi. "It's 10:00 A.M.—Do You Know What Your Sitter's Doing?" Redbook 120 (1997): 144–147.

Cottle, Michelle. "Who's Watching the Kids?" *Washington Monthly* 30, no. 78 (July 1998): 16–26.

Craig, Sharon. "The Effects of an Adapted Interactive Writing, Intervention on Kindergarten Children's Phonological Awareness, Spelling, and Early Reading Development." *Reading Research Quarterly* 38, no 4 (October–December 2003): 438–440.

"Daycares Don't Care." http://www.daycaresdontcare.org/Books/Books_1995–1999_7.htm.

DeSchipper, J. Clauset. "The Relation of Flexible Childcare to Quality of Center

Daycare and Children's Socio-Emotional Functioning." *Infant Behavior and Development* 26, no. 3 (2003): 24–30.

Dillon, Jennifer. "Pay and Benefits Lag at Day Care Centers." *Boston Globe,* 6 February 2002, NH1.

Eberlein, Tamara. "Child Care: What Works Best for Kids. *Redbook* (June 2002): 90–92.

Economic Opportunity Institute. "How Does High Quality Child Care Benefit Business and the Local Economy?" *ExchangeEveryDay,* 9 November 2005. http://childcareexchange.com.

Farrell, Ann. "Building Social Capital in Early Childhood Education and Care: An Australian Study." *British Educational Research Journal* 30, no. 5 (2004): 623–632.

Frones, Ivar. "The Transformation of Childhood." *Acta Sociologica* 40, no. 1 (1997): 17–30.

Futurist. "Investing in Children," 32 (June/July 1998): 15–20.

Galinsky, Ellen. *The Costs of NOT Providing Quality Early Childhood Programs.* Washington, D.C.: National Association for the Education of Young Children, 1996.

Gonzalez-Mena, Janet. *Foundations: Early Childhood Education in a Diverse Society.* Mountain View, Calif.: Mayfield Publishing, 1998.

Hart, Joanna. "Child Care Costs Forcing Reliance on Unlicensed." *Boston Globe,* 22 March 2000, B1.

Killam, Edward. "A Guide to Child Care Services." *FBI Law Enforcement Bulletin* (June 1985): 21–25.

Kisker, E. E., S. Hofferth, D. Phillips, and E. Farquhar. A Profile of Child Care Settings: Early Education and Care in 1990. Vol. 1. Princeton, N.J.: Mathematica Policy Research, Inc. 1991. (ED 343 702).

Klass, Carol. "Social and Familial Childrearing: An Examination of Daycare and the Modern Family." *Journal of Education* 165, no. 4 (1983): 375.

MacQuarrie, Brian. "Day Care Site Shut Over Its Condition." *Boston Globe,* 13 July 2002, B1.

McCartney, Kathleen. "Children Have Fewer Problems at Child Care Centers that Meet Standards." *American Journal of Public Health.* July. 26–9. 1999.

McIntyre, Lee. "Childcare on Board: The Growth of Worksite Daycare." *Digital,* 30 September 2000: 7–8.

Moon, Rachel, Wendy Biliter, and Sarah Croskell. "Examination of State Regulations Regarding Infants and Sleep in Licensed Child Care Centers and Family Child Care Settings." *Pediatrics* 107, no. 5 (May 2001): 1029–1037.

National Child Care Staffing Study. http://www.necic.org/ccb/ccb-s096/research.html.

National Institute of Child Health and Human Development. *Early Child Care*

Research Network. Bethesda, Md.: NICHD, 1998.

New York Times. "Children of Working Poor Are Day Care's Forgotten." 25 November 1997.

———. "Crying Need—Day-Care Quandary: A Nation at War With Itself." Week in Review, 11 January 1998, 18.

———. "Mothers Poised for Workfare Face Acute Lack of Day Care." 14 April 1998, A27.

Oekerman, Rebecca. "Corporate-Sponsored Child Care: Benefits for Children, Families, and Employers." *Early Childhood Education Journal* 25, no. 2 (December 1997): 13–17.

Penn, Helen. "Policy and Practice in Childcare and Nursery Education." *Journal of Social Policy* 29, no. 1 (January 2000): 37–54.

Phillips, Deborah. *Quality in Child Care: What Does Research Tell Us?* Washington, D.C.: National Association for the Education of Young Children, 1993.

Polansky, Norman, Paul Ammons, and Barbara Weathersby. "Is There an American Standard of Child Care?" *Social Work* (September–October 1983): 341–346.

Roseman, Marilyn. "Quality Child Care: At Whose Expense?" *Early Childhood Education Journal* 27, no. 1 (September 1999): 5–11.

Shuster, Kramer. *The Hard Questions in Family Day Care: National Issues and Exemplary Programs.* New York: National Council of Jewish Women Center for the Child, 2001.

Smith, Lynn. "Child Day Care Standards Affirmed." *The Boston Globe,* 11 January 1997, A3.

Swarns, Rachel. "Mothers Poised for Workfare Face Acute Lack of Day Care." *New York Times,* 14 April 1998, A1.

Thompson, Penny, and Nancy Molyneaux. "Enforcing Child Care Standards: Nobody Is Talking About Enforcement: Without It, Standards Are Meaningless." *Public Welfare* 50 (Winter 1992): 20–25.

University of Colorado. *Cost, Quality and Child Outcomes in Child Care Centers.* Denver, Colo.: Center for Research on Economic and Social Policy, 1999.

Vakil, Shernavaz. "The Reggio Emilia Approach and Inclusive Early Childhood Programs." *Early Childhood Education. Journal* 30, no. 3 (March 2003): 187.

Walters, David R. *Casebook in Child Abuse.* Bloomington, Ind.: Indiana University Press, 1969.

———. *Physical and Sexual Abuse of Children.* Bloomington, Ind.: Indiana University Press, 1968.

Wen, Patricia. "Wary Parents Using Cameras, Criminal Checks on Caregivers." *Boston Globe,* 17 July 2000, A1.

Whitebook, Marcy, Laura Saki, Emily Gerber, and Carolle Howes. *Then and*

Now: Changes in Child Care Staffing 1994–2000. Washington, D.C.: Center for Child Care Workforce, 2000.

Young, Kathryn Taaffe, Katherine Marsland, and Edward Zigler. "The Regulatory Status of Center Based Infant and Toddler Child Care." *American Journal of Orthopsychiatry* 67, no. 4 (1997): 535–543.

Zuckerman, Diana. "Childcare Staff: The Lowdown on Salaries and Stability." *Youth Today* (June 2002): 14–16.

Chapter 3 How Safe Are Nannies and Au Pairs?

On the recommendation of a referral agency, Deborah and Sunil Eappen of Newton, Massachusetts, hired an Englishwoman, eighteen-year-old Louise Woodward, to take care of their two sons. Louise was young, inexperienced, and spent too many hours alone with eight-month-old Matthew and his brother. She came to the United States for adventure and enjoyed going out with friends. Often she didn't get home until late, but her workday started early. One fateful day while giving Matthew a bath, she allegedly became annoyed, violently shook him, and then tossed him onto a pile of towels lying on the hard, tiled bathroom floor. He died of a brain hemorrhage and Shaken Baby Syndrome. Louise likely never meant for the child to be hurt; she was tired, immature, and used bad judgment. It was a catastrophe for all involved. A beautiful child was dead, the Eappens lost their son, and Louise went on trial for murder.

Obviously, such an outcome is not what parents expect when they hire nannies or au pairs to watch their children. In-home caregivers are appealing to working parents who don't want to drag children out the door early each morning and who feel that children are better off in their own homes, in their own beds, playing with their own toys, in familiar environments. The challenge of finding a good nanny who is willing to come into the home to care for children is decades old. Where, parents wonder, is Mary Poppins?

Parents who want in-home care often require much more than babysitters; they might need cooks, chauffeurs, housecleaners, teachers, playmates, psychologists, and social secretaries as well. They may place these demands upon the nanny, au pair, or babysitter. When these caregivers live in the home, parents may expect their help even in off-hours; unlike people who leave their work site in order to go home, live-in providers are never fully removed from their job's responsibilities and employer's scrutiny. Well-meaning parents can end up being bad employers because they are unclear about what they expect. They often demand too much, pay too little, interfere with the nanny's instructions to the children, and don't give enough positive reinforcement or personal space. While some caregivers become extensions of the family, more often neither parent nor provider ends up totally happy. In these cases, it's the children who suffer most.

TYPES OF PROVIDERS

Nannies.

The most professional of the in-home child-care providers, nannies traditionally live at the child's home, but day nannies who have their own homes are increasingly common. There are also temporary nannies, such as people hired specifically to take care of the children when the family is on vacation. Nannies are usually well-trained with credentials in child development, health, safety, and nutrition and are well-suited to meet the physical, emotional, intellectual, social, and recreational needs of children. Their duties include child care and minor domestic tasks relating primarily to child care; they may cook for the children, but would not be expected to cook a meal for the household. Nannies manage children's activities, create adventures and outings, and develop opportunities for conceptual and intellectual stimulation. Because they are highly trained professionals, they tend to be expensive. As a result, middle- and lower-class families cannot usually afford a nanny.

The American Council of Nanny Schools reports that most nannies are between the ages of twenty-two and twenty-six, are high school graduates, come from large families, hold traditional gender roles, and have been trained in key child-care concepts. Nannies may also be adult women who don't have children who feel that child care is a suitable occupation or women who have raised their own families but no longer have little ones of their own to care for. These older women tend to be very experienced and more expensive than younger nannies, and their "been there, done that" background makes them good caregivers. There are also international nannies, who are often willing to work for less money because they are eager to stay in the country. They may need more help with language, cultural adjustments, and assistance with immigration authorities, but they tend to be loyal and willing to do domestic tasks that other nannies are less willing to accept.

Use of nannies is common around the world, from Chinese amahs to British child minders. British "nursery nurses" receive over 3,000 hours of extensive formal child-care training, while in the United States, there are no legal requirements for training or qualifications, no national standards, and certification is regulated by individual states. The Professional Association of

Nursery Nannies estimates there are 200,000 nannies with qualifications that range widely, from university, college, or nanny school to high school or less. There are 300 nanny agencies in the United States. According to Mary Clurman, publisher of Nanny News, most check references to ensure the nannies will be safe and appropriate. But other reports indicate that only 10 to 30 percent of agencies do thorough background and criminal record checks on the people they place. Which is true? It depends on the agency.

Once placed, there usually isn't extensive monitoring or evaluation of nannies and au pairs by the agencies. Because there is no official monitoring agency, children cared for at home are often denied the safeguards that apply to care for children in daycare centers, schools, or other institutions and parents are not alerted about which nannies are dangerous. Glowing testimonials for nannies as "godsends" can be found on web sites like www.ilovemynanny.com, yet other families have not found the experience to be positive. Some worried parents have resorted to installing hidden cameras so they can make sure their children are being cared for properly.

Governesses.

A governess is a well-educated person hired to teach school-aged children in the home or on trips to ensure continuity in the children's education. One could regard them as a specially trained type of tutor. Usually governesses don't do cleaning or cooking or provide care for preschool children. Many parents who want household help as well as child care select au pairs.

Au Pairs.

Frequently au pairs are lumped in the same category as nannies, but they aren't the same. The au pair program was developed to enable young people to get international experience while they work off room and board by babysitting. Au pair ads portray the experience in a tantalizing way. The ads imply that au pairs will have time to travel, go to school, and make friends in exchange for babysitting a few hours each week and doing some light housework. Conversely, the au pair experience has not been marketed to parents as a cultural exchange program but as a way to get inexpensive child care. Consequently, au pairs may find themselves frustrated by parents who expect a full-time caregiver and domestic servant and provide them no free time or space for themselves. Parents may be annoyed if au pairs aren't as committed to child care as they anticipated. The mismatch of expectations between parents and au pairs is a recipe for potential disaster.

Au pairs are usually between the ages of eighteen and twenty-six; most are not experienced in taking care of children, which is a problem if parents assume they have such experience. Au pairs are supposed to complete training in child safety and child development, but the specific content of the training isn't standardized, and information like the dangers of shaking a baby could easily be omitted. There is usually no agency supervision after placement, so parents are responsible for monitoring and safety instruction.

Many parents have had generally positive experiences with au pairs. They understood the nature of the au pair program, accepted the developmental issues of young women, and helped the girls to accommodate positively to America. Because these parents knew what they were getting into and communicated with their au pairs to solve problems in supportive ways, they found the au pair program was successful.

In-home babysitters.

Although they may refer to themselves as nannies, in-home babysitters are usually less trained than nannies or au pairs, rely upon personal experience, get paid less, receive no benefits, and are expected to do domestic chores. They are often friends or acquaintances of parents, and babysitters seldom receive as thorough background checks as nannies or au pairs. They vary widely in their competence. Overnight sitters are particularly desired by people who work odd hours or third-shift jobs, because most parents prefer that their children sleep at home in their own beds. Organized daycare programs are less available for parents who work nontraditional jobs, making use of informal, home-based care their only realistic option. Some parents may expect sitters to do housekeeping, cooking, and errands in addition to taking care of kids. While some parents find great sitters to come into their homes, most resort to "the best we can get."

HOW TO CHOOSE A NANNY OR AU PAIR

Decide if you really want a nanny or au pair.

Is someone coming into your home really best for you and your family? It is convenient, but it is also usually more expensive than taking your children out for care. It is also more socially isolating than daycare and requires that kids and providers spend lots of time together.

Pick reputable placement agencies.

Usually parents don't know people who are nannies, au pairs, or in-home sitters, which means they have to find other people to steer them toward providers who will be a good fit. Agencies can help parents to find candidates who look promising. But remember, agencies are businesses that charge money for their services and placements. So be careful, ask questions, and demand information.

Interview applicants yourself.

While agencies can conduct initial screenings of potential nannies and au pairs, taking their endorsements at face-value can be a mistake. Hiring someone sight unseen is unwise. Smart parents will interview the pool of applicants and do further screening if necessary. If you are going to have someone come into your home to live and care for your children, it is worth the effort. Make sure they have first aid training, know how to swim, and have a good driving record. Determine if they will discipline your children in ways you approve, if they will create activities and educational plans that fit your children's needs, and if they will be flexible and responsible.

Sign a contract.

It is useful to clarify, in writing, what you expect, and what you will give in return. A contract enables both parties to discuss different needs and goals and to negotiate a relationship that actually works for both. Don't assume that people can read your mind—put in writing what is and is not acceptable to you.

Try a trial run.

When you hire someone to care for your kids, it can take a while for everyone to work together. This is to be expected, and modifications may need to be made. During this probationary time, close supervision is needed and good communication is essential. If problems continue to exist after a reasonable time has passed and attempts to resolve them have failed, it may be time to find another nanny. Be aware that getting rid of an au pair who doesn't meet your needs may be difficult, especially if they have traveled long distances for your job. Many parents have found that when they constructively confronted problems early on and created workable options, inexperienced au pairs could be taught how to become excellent caregivers.

Offer good pay and benefits.

While verbal encouragement is nice, workers prefer raises and bonuses. Nannies and au pairs may expect to receive insurance, healthcare coverage, educational assistance, and retirement compensation. All employees need to feel valued. Gifts and paid vacations will help them to keep their enthusiasm and commitment high.

Keep a watchful eye, but don't be paranoid.

As Matthew Eppan's parents learned the hard way, all providers must receive constant supervision and monitoring. This is especially true when nannies and au pairs are young and inexperienced. Parents and providers must communicate with each other about what is working and change situations that aren't. It is better to confront problems when they are small then when they accumulate and escalate. If parents feel suspicious enough to install hidden video cameras to monitor what goes on while they are away, their intuition is telling them that there is a potential of risk. In these cases, it is probably time to look for another provider.

PROMISING PROGRAMS

There are a variety of agencies and organizations that seek to help parents find qualified workers. The million-dollar business that has been built around placement of nannies and au pairs means that if the agencies do poor-quality work, the agencies may go out of business. These organizations, listed in the following resource list show parents what to look for when hiring help. The internet, too, has become an extremely valuable resource for helping kids, parents, and providers.

RESOURCES

America's Nannies
PO Box 9151
Paramus, NJ 07653
(888) 626-6437
http://www.americasnannies.com

Ask Nanny
http://ask-nanny.com/childcare.html

Au Pair in America
River Plaza
9 West Broad Street
Stamford, CT 06902
(800) 928-7247 or (203) 399-5000
http://www.aupairinamerica.com

Au Pair USA
161 Sixth Ave.
New York, NY 10013
(800) AUPAIRS or (212) 924-0446
http://www.aupairusa.org

Everything Nanny
550 Brick Blvd.
Brick, NJ 08723
(866) 296-2669
http://www.4nanny.com/benefits.shtml

International Au Pair Association
IAPA Secretariat
Bredgade 25 H
1260 Copenhagen K
Denmark
+45 3317 0066
http://www.iapa.org

International Nanny Association
2020 Southwest Freeway, Suite 208
Houston, TX 77098
(888) 878-1477 or (713) 526-2670
http://www.nanny.org

Nanny Network
Home/Work Solutions, Inc.
2 Pigeon Hill Dr., # 550
Sterling, VA 20165
(800) 626-4829
www.nannynetwork.com

National Association of Nannies
25 Route 31 South, Suite C
Pennington, NJ 08534
(800) 344-6266
http://www.nannyassociation.com

United States Department of State
Au Pairs
301 4th St., SW
Room 820
Washington, DC 20547
(202) 203-5029
http://exchanges.state.gov/education/
jexchanges/private/aupair.htm

REFERENCES

Ackerman, Elise. "Workfare Mary Poppins: Should Welfare Moms Take Care of Other People's Kids?" *U.S. News and World Report* 123, no. 3 (1997): 36–37.

Bassett, Monica. *The Professional Nanny.* New York: Delmar Publishers, 1998.

Boppett, Trish. *The Nanny Chronicles,* 2002. http://citypaper.net/articles/2002-05-30/cover.shtml. 2002.

Carlton, Susan, and Coco Myers. *The Nanny Book: The Smart Parent's Guide to Hiring, Firing, and Every Sticky Situation in Between.* New York: St. Martins, 1999.

Court TV Online. "*Massachusetts v Woodward:* The Nanny Trial." http://www.courttv.com/trials/woodward.

Fildes, Valerie. *Wet Nursing: A History of Antiquity to the Present.* Boston: Blackwell Publishers, 1988.

Foote, David. "Staffing Problems? Learn From the Nanny Dilemma." 11

December 2000.
http://www.computerworld.com.

Griffith, Susan, and Sharon Legg. *The Au Pair and Nanny's Guide*. Oxford: Vacation Work Publications, 2002.

Lillywhite, Vinnie. *Guilt By Suspicion*. Bloomington, Ind.: AuthorHouse, 2000.

Matthews, Hilli. *Successful Au Pairs*. London: Sheldon Press, 2001.

Moninger, Jeanette. "Ready For Life With Mary Poppins?" http://www.babyzone.com/features/content/display.asp?TopicID=9173&ContentID=1503.

Moon, Rachel, Buce Sprague, and Kantilal Patel. "Stable Prevalence but Changing Risk Factors for Sudden Infant Death Syndrome in Child Care Settings in 2001." *Pediatrics*, 116, no. 4 (October 2005): 972–977.

Pekkanen, Sarah. "Searching for Mary Poppins." http://www.washingtonian.com/etc/shopping/nannies.html.

Raffin, Michele. *The Good Nanny Book*. New York: Berkeley Publishing Group, 1996.

Wikipedia. "Louise Woodward." http://en.wikipedia.org/wiki/Louise_Woodward.

Wolfe, Jerri. *Redbook's Nannies, Au Pairs & Babysitters: How to Find and Keep the Right In-Home Child Care for Your Family*. New York: Hearst, 2001.

Chapter 4 Child Care by Family and Friends Relative Safety

Bryan loved his mother but didn't want her to babysit his infant daughter and toddler son. He knew she enjoyed reading stories and playing games with them, and the kids loved her. But he remembered the times she lost her temper. He recalled being smacked, pinched, and called names in order to get him to "behave." Bryan thought his mom was scatterbrained and used poor judgment. She gave the kids foods he didn't want them to have, she sometimes used bad language around them, and Bryan didn't approve of all her friends who stopped by. He detested her driving. Although he felt it was important for the kids to have a relationship with their grandma, Bryan concluded that he could not allow his mother to care for his children unless he or his wife was present.

Ashley and Tracey, mothers of three-year-old children, decided to swap child care during their back-to-back doctor appointments. While Tracey was with the doctor, the kids happily played with Ashley. But when Ashley went to her appointment, Tracey chatted to others in the waiting room and paid more attention to her daughter than Ashley's son. When the little boy began frothing at the mouth, she realized that he had put a small ball into his mouth and was choking. Tracey started screaming and was incapable of doing anything to help the child. Another woman who saw what was happening calmly worked with the little boy while another woman dialed 911. Ashley heard the commotion and discovered her son could have died, because the woman she trusted to watch him hadn't.

Did Bryan overreact or take reasonable steps to protect his children? It is difficult to determine, since the situation is influenced by the fact that the caregiver is his mother. Should Ashley allow Tracey to watch her children again? Often, family and friends are often held to different standards than other providers.

The most commonly used child-care providers are family and friends. This model of care continues to be many parents' first choice. This is because parents expect their friends and family to love, and therefore protect, their children. Heartwarming stereotypes of children baking cookies with Grandma, fishing with Grandpa, or playing with cousins entice parents toward family-based child care. Other parents rely on family and friends to provide child care because they tend to be less expensive and more convenient than daycare or nannies. Soaring costs, nontraditional work hours, and long daycare waiting lists have given parents few alternatives except turning to relatives, friends, and acquaintances to watch their children.

Two-thirds of children in the United States are left in informal settings where parents have no way of knowing for sure whether their children receive the kind of attention they need. Few relatives and friends are licensed or certified, and most rely upon experience to guide them when interacting with kids. They generally don't develop educational plans or activities for the children and take a more relaxed attitude toward caregiving. When parents purchase care from daycare centers, they expect competence and educational activities for their children; when parents get care from family and friends, they primarily expect their children will be loved and amused. This is an important distinction. Parents must weigh the values of love, convenience, and competence. They must also consider whether education or recreation is more important for their children. "It's not that there is something right or wrong with informal care. It is that there are no standards," cautions Doug Baird, president of Associated Day Care Services. The lack of training, supervision, and accountability in informal child-care providers puts kids in more potentially risky situations than with any other type of provider.

Use of family and friends to watch over children may be convenient, but it can also be stress-producing for both parents and caregivers. When asked to take care of children, many family members and friends do so reluctantly. Adults have schedules to keep, relationships that require their ongoing attention, and activities they want to pursue. Interjecting a child into that equation may put even the most beloved child in a less-than-perfect care situation. Friends and family may agree to watch children more out of obligation than desire: Over 60 percent of relatives who care for children said they only did so "to help out the mother."

Parents and their relatives or friends may have conflicting ideas about childrearing. Although they share mutual bonds of concern and affection, they may have drastically different beliefs about how to discipline kids. Parents may feel uncomfortable asking family members or friends to change their behavior, fearing that, if they complain, their relationships with family and friends may be jeopardized. As a result, parents may not express their concerns. This leaves their children at risk.

TYPES OF INFORMAL CAREGIVERS

Grandparent care.

Grandparents are the most used informal care provider, with 1.4 million providing daycare or evening care to their grandchildren. Having grandchildren is typically regarded as one of life's joys for most adults, and they look forward to being with them. They have an emotional bond with the kids, tend to be reliable, and parents know from personal experience what to expect. University of Oxford professor Sarah Harper found that 75 percent of parents rely on their own parents at some time for care and believe their parents will help them eagerly and gladly. However, she also learned that while grandparents, friends, and other family members love the children, caring for them is frequently an imposition. Grandparents do not know how to tell their children that the burden of care is sometimes too much, especially when it is expected and unpaid. People are happy to help out but not to be taken for granted. Grandparents assume that watching kids will be a temporary arrangement. While excited initially, they grow resentful of ongoing demands, especially if more grandchildren are born and added to their burden of care. One grandmother confided that, "It was wonderful at first . . . but that was ten years and three children ago, and . . . I'm tired, I can't cope, and I can't say no because it might cause such bad feelings that she would stop me seeing them at all." Grandparents vary widely in age, interests, and ability, and so does their ability to care for kids. Parents know their own parents' strengths and limitations, and they should bracket their children's time with them to ensure their children's safety without hurting their parents' feelings.

Cousin, aunt, and other relative care.

Families rely upon their extended network for support and help. Usually female relatives are contacted, but uncles or other male relatives may also be asked to "babysit." Sometimes cousins will have children who are around the same age, so stay-at-home relatives may suddenly find they have a bunch of little ones to watch. Many families have an aunt who is the designated caregiver for the family. This family network can be great for kids, but it is difficult for a cousin or aunt to turn away another family member's request for help. It is hard for parents to confront relatives when they aren't happy with some aspect of care, and it is equally difficult for the relative to confront parents when they aren't paid or when they feel they are asked to do too much.

Care by friends and acquaintances.

Parents naturally build a social network that consists of other parents who have children approximately the same age. It is convenient to opt for friend-delivered care, especially when care from family is not available. Besides having someone to watch your child, there are emotional benefits to letting your child make friends with the children of your friends, who are likely to value the same kinds of things that you do. Friends may swap child care without the exchange of money unless child care is provided on a regular basis for extended periods of time. While friendships may vary in intensity, usually they are less emotionally charged than those with family members, which make it easier to talk frankly about child care issues. However, it is still hard to negotiate care because of the socio-emotional link among the parents.

Babysitters.

Almost everyone hires babysitters; some people use sitters once in a while, others for all day, many for several days each week. While anyone can be a sitter, most tend to be young and female and are usually acquaintances of the parents. Sitters are desirable because they tend to have flexible schedules, they're not expensive compared to daycare centers, and they often will do tasks that are beyond the regular scope of caregiving activities. Drawbacks to using sitters are that they tend to be inexperienced and may lack the maturity to make good decisions, especially in a crisis. Because friendships are very important for teenagers, some sitters may talk on the phone or have visits from friends, which could interfere with their care of children.

Care by families of your children's friends.

As children develop friendships, and visit with their friends, their friends' parents will occasionally oversee your child, just as you will be put in the position of caring for other parents' kids. Often, we don't know much about these people, and they don't know much about us. It is awkward to interview such people about how attentive they are to safety. Most parents walk their children into another person's home when they drop them off to take a quick scan for cleanliness, safety, and signs of order or distress. Many will gingerly inquire about things like, "Are you going to stay with the kids while they're swimming?" or "Are you skating at the pond? The ice hasn't looked very thick lately." Risks vary for children according to age; the younger the children, the more closely their care must be monitored. For instance, at sleepovers, kids may get exposed to the consumption of tobacco or alcohol, inappropriate movies, or fights. Conversely, they may witness acts of generosity, humor, and kindness. The issue is that you don't know, but you must try to get a sense of the situation. As children get older, parents should continue to monitor where they are.

What all of these informal providers have in common is a relationship in which the parent expects that others will proactively care about their children. The sense of obligation influences the ability of the friend or relative to say "no." When adults don't have the time, interest, resources, or desire to watch over other people's children, they are less likely to do a good job, which increases risk. Parents are therefore put in the tough position of sorting through what the providers say and what they mean when it comes to their stated willingness to watch their children.

HOW TO CHOOSE FAMILY AND FRIENDS AS CHILD-CARE PROVIDERS

It is possible that family and friends will be good caregivers, but here are some issues to consider:

Decide if you really want to use family and friends as caregivers.
This question is a critically important one for parents to answer. There are benefits and drawbacks to any type of child care, especially care by family and friends. Parents shouldn't create fantasies about how perfect grandma- or auntie-delivered care may be. They should look objectively at potential problems, as well as benefits that their children may receive from informal care. People who are too young, too sick, or too old simply may not be able to watch children carefully enough to ensure their safety. Also, children's needs change as they get older, so while staying with Grandma may be fun when the children are young, older children may prefer other types of care. Sometimes it is much easier to arrange appropriate care with professionals.

Find out if your friends and family really want to babysit your children.
Parents who ask family and friends to watch their children may find that they reluctantly agree when they really want to decline. If family and friends aren't really invested in being caregivers, children may not receive high-quality care, but it is difficult for people who have an emotionally close bond

to deny others what they want. Watching children is hard work, and the hours of care that are needed may exceed the number of hours that friends or family can realistically give. Family and friends are likely not to ask parents for money because of their affectionate bond, but they actually would like to be paid well for their time and effort if care is provided on a regular basis.

Can you check references of family and friends?

Sure, but not in the same way as one would with a total stranger. When dealing with family and friends, doing background checks can be a little trickier than other types of screening. Ask other parents if they've been comfortable with the care. Don't sacrifice an important emotional relationship by turning it a business one. Most informal care providers are not trained, and their homes are not licensed; in fact, they are usually exempt from state regulations. Parents are on their own when making sure care is of high quality.

Do you approve of their discipline?

Research shows that relatives and friends generally use harsher discipline than strangers because their emotional investment in the child is higher than that of an outsider. Family members may use strict discipline on children because they regard it as a deterrent for misbehavior later in life. They may view a child's misbehavior as a reflection of themselves and vigorously discipline a child because they don't want to be embarrassed. Studies indicate it is much more likely that a child will be physically, sexually, or emotionally abused by relatives or close family friends than non-family caretakers, such as a child-care worker, teacher or counselors.

Assess potential for accidents, negligence and poor judgment.

Love doesn't necessarily equal good care. Family and friends may love your little ones, but if they're not prepared and are providing care out of obligation, this increases risk. Take a normally busy adult schedule, add children into the equation, and loving adults may find themselves overloaded with too much to do and too little time and energy to do it. As a result, accidents are likely to occur, such as the Philadelphia grandfather who left his infant granddaughter in the car while he went to work, forgetting that he had to drop her at the babysitter's house. The temperature in the car reached 140 degrees, and the girl died. Because adults are overwhelmed with their own responsibilities, children may be accidentally put into harm's way; examples include kids who get burned or start fires, run into the street and get hit by cars, fall into the pool and drown, or play with guns. In 2000 almost 2,000 children under the age of fourteen were treated in hospital emergency rooms for unintentional firearm-related injuries. The list of life-threatening, preventable accidents goes on. Usually no one finds out about the near-misses.

Know what they're doing.

Parents need to know what their children are doing when they are with caregivers. Many children in informal care watch several hours of television each day, are taken on other people's errands, or are left to entertain themselves. Conversely, others learn valuable skills, like Robert, who helped remodel his uncle's house. Robert learned how to negotiate purchases at the hardware store and how to measure, cut, hammer, nail, and create a finished product while he listened to family stories. This was an educational and affectionate experience that helped create a warm bond between the boy and his uncle.

Be sensitive to everyone's needs, including your own.

Be clear about what you expect from the caregiver, and anticipate that your friends and family members will tell you what they need and want. The only way that family- and friend-delivered child care can work successfully is when everyone is communicating effectively. Family and friends do parents a favor by watching their children. They may not do things exactly the way parents may prefer. Parents may find they must overlook some actions if they want to preserve their relationship. But parents have the responsibility to make sure basic care is met and that their kids are safe, even with best friends or relatives.

Create an environment for problem-solving.

Caring for kids is a partnership. Everyone parents differently, even people in the same family. Assume that there will be differences of opinion on how to care for children. Confronting loved ones is difficult. Using a nonadversarial, nondefensive problem solving style will help parents and caregivers to create options. Sometimes, one option may be for the friend or family member to stop providing child care. Usually, it is clear to everyone when a situation needs to change. Exiting the caregiving situation smoothly is important if you want to preserve the emotional relationship with family and friends.

PROMISING PROGRAMS

Informal care is a major form of child care and should receive more public attention. Due to the major increase in the number of grandparents who watch their grandchildren, there has been a social movement to empower them and give them more rights. Organizations like the American Association of Retired Persons (AARP) have been advocates for grandparents receiving support as they care for their grandchildren. This has opened communication between parents and grandparents about the details of how care is delivered and appropriate forms of financial reimbursement. This advocacy network was created as a result of problems grandparents experienced in their role as caregivers; they were responsible for child care but lacked the recognition or authority to provide all aspects of care. As a result of their frustration, they turned to the courts and social service network. At the other end of the spectrum, there is now a national effort to teach young people about to become better babysitters. Courses are offered by cooperative extensive services, social service agencies, religious organizations, or libraries and are designed to teach young people how to care for children's basic needs and what to do in case of an emergency. The model of communities working together as partners to address the needs of children and providers is effective and improves the quality of childcare.

RESOURCES

American Association for Retired Persons
Grandparent Information Center
601 E Street, NW
Washington, DC 20049
(888) 637-2277
http://www.AARP.org

American Self Help Clearinghouse
City University of New York
365 Fifth Avenue, Suite 3300
New York, NY 10016
(212) 817-1822
http://www.selfhelpgroups.org

Associated Day Care Services
95 Berkley Street, Suite 306
Boston, MA 02116
(617) 695-0700
http://www.associateddaycare.org

Grandparent Caregivers: A National Guide
Institute for Global Communications
PO Box 29047
San Francisco, CA 94120
(415) 561-6355
http://www.igc.org/justice/cjc/lspc/manual/cover.html

Grandparents as Parents
Colorado State University
Fot Collins, CO 80523
(970) 491-1794
http://www.ext.colostate.edu/pubs/
consumer/10241.html

Intergenerational Connections
Florida Department of Elder Affairs
4040 Esplanade Way
Tallahassee, FL 32399
(850) 414-2000
http://www.elderaffairs.state.fl.us

Ohio State University
Grandparents as Parents Again
154 W. 17th Ave.
Columbus, OH 43210
(614) 292-OHIO
http://ohioline.osu.edu/ss-fact/
0157.html

Second Time Around Parents
Child Welfare League of America
440 First Street, NW, 3rd Floor
Washington, DC 20001
(202) 638-2952
www.cwla.org/programs/kinship/
thereoughttobealaw.htm

United States Department of Health and
Human Services
Prevent Child Abuse America
500 N. Michigan Ave., Suite 200
Chicago, IL 60611
(312) 663-3520
http://www.preventchildabuse.org

REFERENCES

Aarmas, G. "American Grandparents Are Filing Care Void for Working Parents." *Associated Press Worldstream*, 31 July 2002.

American Academy of Child and Adolescent Psychiatry. *Children and Firearms*, 1999. http://www.aacap.org.

Archibold, Randal. "Parents Are Charged After Party For Teenagers Includes a Stripper." *New York Times*, 6 September 2001, A24.

BabyCenter. "My Friend Thinks I Should Watch Her Kids For Free." http://bbs.babycenter.com/board/baby/babychildcare/6346/thread/2777894.

Babysitters.com. "Finding a Good Sitter." http://www.babysitters.com.

Baird, Doug. *Day Care*. Associated Day Care Services. http://www.associated daycare.org.

Brandon, Peter D. "An Analysis of Kin-Provided Child Care in the Context of Intrafamily Exchanges: Linking Components of Family Support for Parents Raising Young Children." *American Journal of Economics and Sociology* 59, no. 2 (April 2000): 191.

Brown, Harriet. *Babysitter's Handbook.* Middleton, Wisc.: American Girl, 1999.

Casper, Lynne. "Who's Minding Our Preschoolers?" *Current Population Reports.* U.S. Department of the Census. Washington, D.C.: Government Printing Office, 1997.

Christian, Nichole. "Woman Is Accused of Taking Pornographic Photos of Children." *New York Times,* 23 February 2002, A15.

Common Sense About Kids and Guns. "Gun Accidents, Suicides Increase Among Kids." 11 October 2000. http://www.kidsandguns.org/study/inthenews.asp?ID=419.

Daly, Daniel, and Thomas Dowd. "Characteristics of Effective, Harm-Free Environment for Children in Out of Home Care." *Child Welfare* 71, no. 6 (December 1992): 486–496.

Finkelhor, David. "Crimes Against Children by Babysitters." *Juvenile Justice Bulletin.* http://www.ncjrs.gov/html/ojjdp/jjbul2001_9_4/contents.html.

Fiore, Michael. "Near Drowning." http://www.emedicine.com/ped/topic2570.htm.

Fromm, Suzette. "Total Estimated Cost of Child Abuse and Neglect in the U.S.: Third National Incidence Study." 2000. www.preventchildabuse.org/learn_more/research_docs/cost_analysis.pdf.

Galinksy, Ellen. *The Study of Children in Family Child Care and Relative Care: Highlights of Findings.* Washington, D.C.: Families and Work Institute, 1994.

Goodfellow, Joy. "Grandparents Supporting Working Families." http://www.aifs.gov.au/institute/pubs/fm2003/fm66/jg.pdf.

Harding, Jim. "Parentalk." *The Guide to Being a Grandparent.* London: Challenge, 2002.

Hayman, Suzie. "It's Too Much Too Late in Life." *The Times,* 18 February 2002.

Kids and Cars. "Heat Related Hyperthermia News." http://www.kidsandcars.org/incidents/heat.html.

Kids Health. "Choosing and Instructing a Babysitter." http://kidshealth.org/parent/positive/family/babysitter.html.

Kids in Cars. "Mother's Boyfriend Accused in Baby's Death." http://www.kidsincars.org/actualcases/Hyperthermia.htm.

Kontos, Susan. *Quality in Family Child Care and Relative Care.* Washington, D.C.: Families and Work Institute, 1994.

Kornheiser, Tony. "Before You Take Algebra You Need Sums." *Washington Post,* 23 September 2005. http://www.clearlight.com/~jtrosen/tony_stuff/september232001.htm.

Mader, S. "Understand Your Support Systems." *Family Tapestry,* Columbus: Ohio State University Extension, 1998.

Margolin, Leslie. "Abuse and Neglect in Nonparental Child Care: A Risk Assessment." *Journal of Marriage and the Family* 53 (August 1991): 694–704.

Powers, Julie. *Not Just A Babysitter: Making Childcare Work For You.* St. Paul, Minn.: Readleaf Press, 2005.

Rivas, Lynn May. "We Are Not Babysitters: Family Child Care Providers Redefine Work and Care." *Social Forces* 267 (March 2005).

Safe Kids. "Facts About Childhood Drowning." 2006. http://www.usa. safekids.org/content_documents/ Drowning_facts.pdf.

Schuster, Mark. "Unlocked Guns in Many U.S. Homes With Kids." *American Journal of Public Health* (March 2000).

Smith, A. "Investing in Family." *Family Tapestry.* Columbus: Ohio State University Extension, 1998.

Stemmel, Andrew. "The Perceived Benefits and Problems Associated with Intergenerational Exchanges in Day Care." *Gerontologist* 34, no. 4 (1994): 513.

Takas, M. *Grandparents Raising Grandchildren.* New York: Brookdale Foundation Group, 1995.

Tassy, Elaine. "Around-the-Clock Child Care." *The Baltimore Sun,* 28 June 1998, F1.

University of Michigan. "*Safety:* Kids and Guns." http://www.med.umich.edu/ 1libr/yourchild/guns.htm.

"Welcome to Grandparenthood." Age Concern. http:// www.ageconcern.org.uk/ageconcern/ staying_1158.htm.

Whitaker, Barbara. "Boy's Body Found in Pool Police Never Entered." *New York Times,* 6 June 2002, A23.

Chapter 5 Abuse of Children in Religious Organizations

When I was sixteen, I volunteered to be a counselor at a church camp. Many parents expect that their children will be better cared for at a religiously run institution than at a secular facility, because they believe that religious people must be good. This is not always the case. Everything at camp went smoothly until one day while I was on a break I ran into a young man—a minister and the camp's main counselor. We sat alone in the loveliness of the rustic chapel in a moment of respite from the campers. The smiling minister talked about the love of the Lord bringing us all together. He saw me as a special child of God, and I felt uplifted when he held my face in his hands and really looked into my eyes. Suddenly and unexpectedly, he pulled me closer and kissed me. His tongue went into my mouth, one of his hands cupped my breast, and the other slid down my back and into my panties. Aghast, I broke free and ran out of the chapel. Heart pounding, I didn't know what to do. I wondered if I had done something wrong, but I knew I hadn't. I thought about telling someone, but he was part of the camp's administration, and I doubted that anyone would believe me, because it would be my word against his. I ran into another counselor my age, explained what happened, and even my friend couldn't believe that the minister would do such a thing. So I said nothing, kept my distance, and made sure I was never alone during the remainder of my time at camp. To this day, I kept his behavior secret. I was afraid that somehow I would be blamed, that no one would believe what happened, and that nothing would happen to the beloved minister anyway.

It used to be unthinkable that children could be harmed by people in positions of religious authority. People of faith are presumed to act in an exemplary fashion. In recent years we have learned about abuse by priests, but religion teachers, deacons, cantors, staff, and congregation members have also used their access to children to abuse them. Religious organizations have been charged with allowing abuse to occur. Sadly, parents can no longer assume that just because people are religious they are safe around children.

Few authoritative statistics are available on the number and types of child maltreatment by persons in positions of religious authority. When allegations

of clergy abuse exist, the church has a vested interest to keep the allegations secret. But, as the recent sexual abuse scandals in the American Catholic Church
attest, the abuse of children within religious organizations is more than most
people suspected. The Reverend Andrew Greeley estimated that at least 2,500
priests had abused 100,000 victims nationwide since the issue of pedophile
priests first publicly surfaced in 1985, when a Louisiana priest, Gilbert Gauthe,
confessed to molesting dozens of children. Until then, no church had faced litigation for its role in child abuse. But the Father John Geoghan case was a wa-
tershed event, exposing a pedophilic priest crisis when 130 people (mostly
men) came forward to charge him with abuse over a thirty-year period of time.
Child abuse is likely present in religious organizations in every part of the country and every part of the world. From Dallas to Minneapolis, Los Angeles to New
York, and cities in between like Chicago, St. Louis, and Cleveland, there are allegations of clergy sexual abuse. Priests have also been accused of pedophilia in
countries like Ireland, Australia, Canada, Spain, and Mexico.

Studies compiled by the Center for the Prevention of Sexual and Domestic
Violence in Seattle suggest that 15 percent of clergy members in all religious
groups have engaged in some type of inappropriate sexual conduct, from stolen kisses to intercourse. Alan Cooperman, a *Washington Post* journalist, asserts that almost all of America's 178 Catholic dioceses have faced lawsuits
over child abuse. Attorney Jeffrey Anderson's firm in St. Paul gets up to two
hundred calls a day from clergy-abuse survivors. Sylvia Demarest, a Dallas
lawyer, claims that at least 1,500 priests have been publicly accused of sexual
abuse over the past twenty years. But the Catholic Church isn't the only religious organization to confront allegations of misconduct with children. Attorney Joyce Seelen has handled fifty cases of clerical abuse, including Metho-
dists, Episcopalians, Church of Christ, and the Church of the Nazarene.
Charismatic Orthodox Rabbi Baruch Lanner, director of Regions of the National Conference of Synagogue Youth, abused teenagers in his charge over
the course of twenty years, and cantor Howard Nevison in Manhattan turned
himself into authorities after being charged with child molestation. In
Macon, Georgia, Dwight York, founder of the United Nuwaubian Nation of
Moors, was charged with transporting over thirty children ages four to eighteen across state lines for sex and molesting some on trips to Disney World.
Researchers indicate that for every clergy abuse case that is public and legal,
many more are settled quietly or denied. This leads to the conclusion that
clergy abuse of children may be widespread.

Clergy abuse has gone unidentified for many reasons. We have been taught to trust clergy members, and their abuse of children violates the foundations of how we think clergy members are supposed to behave. Clergy, as a professional group, are self-monitored and supervised; no outside regulating body has had the authorization to conduct internal reviews of the behavior or staff in religious organizations or to review their organizational policies and practices. Fearful to disclose abuse, religious leaders have protected themselves and the way they run their organizations. Many religious groups inadequately screen their ministers or church workers and provide few safeguards to prevent negligence or abuse.

Sometimes it is easy to forget about the other people within religious organizations with whom children may have contact. These include teachers, custodians, aides, secretaries, committee leaders, and, of course, congregants. The people over whom the religious organization has the least control are members of the congregation. The open-door policy of religious organizations encourages acceptance of anyone who wishes to worship. This makes it difficult for administrators to ensure absolute safety of the children in the congregation.

When abuse has occurred, perpetrators may protect themselves by redirecting attention away from their act or blaming the victims. Sexually abused children have been encouraged to keep their abuse a secret, ostensibly so others don't view them as "bad" or punish them. Physical assaults on children have been rationalized as necessary to keep children from engaging in what some religious leaders view as sinful behavior. For instance, if children steal, lie, or are sexually active, adults may feel justified in punishing them for violating the Ten Commandments. Sexual contact may be defined as something other than abuse, such as when Christopher Reardon performed oral sex on boys to "educate them," or when Father David Holley molested boys to "teach them how to become men." Patrick Schiltz, a professor at St. Thomas School of Law, found that priests were very clever at avoiding detection. Most, like Ronald Paquin, never defined themselves as pedophiles or predators, even when they exploited children regularly. Clergy like Paul Shanley labeled children as seducers in order to take the focus off his behavior.

Child maltreatment is sometimes kept quiet because people are not sure how to reconcile clergy misconduct with other religious tenets. Some religious principles, such as avoiding malicious gossip, have contributed to discouraging official reporting of adult maltreatment of children. The mandates of forgiveness and redemption have been used to discourage people from reporting perpetrators to the authorities. But turning to confession, prayer, and God may not protect children as effectively as turning to the police and the legal system.

Religious people ignore and deny abuse because they are afraid the church's reputation, funding, or staffing may suffer if the abuses are publicly known. When congregation members lose faith in the church, they are less likely to attend, less likely to volunteer their time, and less likely to donate money. Many religions have a shortage of clergy, and leaders are fearful that prospective clergy members may turn to other occupations if they are too concerned that public suspicion could put them at risk of abuse allegations. Sometimes clergy abuse has been kept a secret because members are afraid the church may be forced to close, which indeed has occurred in Massachusetts. Clergy have relied upon the First Amendment, which is designed to protect freedom of religion, to avoid reporting abuse or handing over documents that may implicate themselves.

The efforts of newspapers, such as the *Boston Globe*, brought the public's attention to the existence of clergy abuse. Legal prosecution of perpetrators and financial settlements for millions of dollars have induced victims to come forward to disclose prior abuse. While some churches have gone bankrupt in an attempt to pay restitution to victims, it gives congregants the clear message that abuse will not be tolerated. Because many victims were young when the abuse occurred and unable to prosecute their perpetrators, statute of limitation laws have made it difficult for them to prosecute their offenders. Victim organizations such as Survivors' Network of those Abused by Priests (SNAP), Voice of the Faithful in Massachusetts, Network of People Abused by Priests in St. Louis, or Kentucky victims' organization Linkup have empowered people who were abused by clergy to have a voice, even when they are unable to receive restitution in a court of law.

ABUSE WITHIN RELIGIOUS ORGANIZATIONS

Types of abuse.

Clergy abuse may technically be no different than any other type of abuse, but the emotional impact is greater because religious leaders are held to a higher standard. Abuse may be sexual, as in the cases of abuse by pedophile priests, but children may also be physically or emotionally abused. Physical assaults are perpetuated by clergy who feel to "spare the rod is to spoil the child." Children can suffer emotional abuse by clergy members who put "the fear of God into them" to make them feel guilty or sinful. Sometimes the different types of abuse are linked together, as in the case of children who are sexually abused and are fearful to tell, even decades later, because of shame and guilt.

Common victims of clergy abuse.

There are certain categories of children that are more frequent victims of clergy abuse than other children. These include:

Altar boys and girls. Children who work closely with priests to prepare for services are more likely to be victimized because they spend unsupervised time together. Bonds of respect, authority, and affection are nurtured in the priest–altar boy/altar girl relationship, which make it harder for children to challenge inappropriate behavior. The trust relationship interferes with children exposing inappropriate clergy behavior because, as James Klemenz of Kentucky recalls, "There is no way in hell my parents would have believed the priest abused me. They were very religious. I might as well have told them a Martian landed in my back yard."

Children who need help. Children who need special attention have been targets for abuse. These include children in single-parent families, children in homes that have economic problems, and those children who need extra emotional and social support. Children who experience conflicts at home, including divorce, alcoholic parents, or domestic violence, may develop relationships with church personnel, perhaps as a buffer for troubles. Because they are vulnerable, these children are easy targets for abusers.

Faithful, compliant children and parents. Quiet children who do what they are told are easy targets for abuse; all abusers tend to avoid children who are outspoken. Abusive clergy members are more likely to prey on families who they perceive will not prosecute them; they look for compliant children with parents who are likely to forgive abuse and pray for the perpetrator.

Effects of abuse on victims.

Children who are abused by clergy experience the same kinds of short- and long-term effects as any other victim of abuse, but the impact is more intense for many children because their abusers were regarded as representatives of God. The fact that religious people have hurt them has resulted in many abused children turning away from religion altogether. Fewer than a quarter of clergy-abused children report their abuse to authorities; most are embarrassed and fear that others won't believe them. As adults, they have high rates of problematic marriages, depression, flashbacks, feelings of worthlessness, alcoholism and drug abuse, sexual dysfunction, guilt, self-destructive behaviors, and suicidal ideation. Boys who are sexually abused may molest children when they become men, perpetuating the cycle of abuse; many pedophile priests were molested when they were children and go on to abuse boys who are the same age as they were when they were molested. Victims of child sexual abuse are often angry that their parents did not protect them. Abuse can also lead to pent-up rage, as seen when Catholic priest Maurice Blackwell was shot by a man who had been abused or when Father John Geoghan was beaten to death in prison.

Types of abusers.

The most common perpetrators in religious organizations include:

Clergy. Child-abuse research indicates that abusers can come from any social class, occupation, race, or age group. Well-adjusted clergy members may be wonderful role models for children, but those with problems may misuse their positions of authority to meet their own needs. Clergy who have relationship issues, personal problems, sexual dysfunctions, substance abuse problems, or who have been victims of abuse themselves are more likely to be abusive when in authoritative positions with unfettered access to children.

Religious school teachers. Since most religious school teachers are volunteers and don't undergo rigorous background investigations, they may be abusive. In order to instill values, many religious school teachers have not allowed frivolous behavior, demanded compliance, shown little tolerance for rule violators, and engaged in corporal punishment. Their competence and motivation varies widely.

Volunteers. For religious organizations that need their help to run programs and functions, volunteers pose a special area of concern. Unlike employees, most volunteers are not subject to extensive background checks. They may be appointed to tasks because of their willingness to work; if they feel others don't trust them, they may threaten not to help at all. Pedophiles have easily slipped into positions with access to children at religious organizations, because leaders usually don't screen volunteers or confront odd behavior.

Congregants. As congregants, people feel they are members of a "family" or exclusive social club. Religious organizations have an open membership policy, which means they must welcome anyone who wants to attend. Congregation members may not share the same values, and they may not know one another well, especially in large organizations. Children interact with a variety of adults at religious services, community services, or recreational and social events. Communities of faith trust that members will act appropriately; as a result safeguards are sometimes not put into place. It is virtually impossible to monitor every interaction a child has with an adult within religious organizations.

HOW TO IDENTIFY SAFE RELIGIOUS COMMUNITIES

On the surface, most religious organizations look like safe and spiritual places. But often they look that way because that is what people expect to see. The following are things that parents can look for to give them an indication whether the church has taken adequate safety precautions for children.

Is there a covenant to protect kids?

Some churches have developed formal statements in which they commit themselves to the care and protection of children. If your religious organization has done this, it is a good sign that they have instituted appropriate safeguards to protect children.

Find out how people who work with children are screened and supervised.

Whether at vacation Bible school, religion classes, or social events, screening and supervision of people working with kids are paramount to the prevention of child abuse. Are only clergy members screened, or do thorough background checks include other paid employees, teachers, and volunteers? If people aren't adequately screened, there may be no reason to distrust them, but there is also no reason to assume that they will be good with children. All workers, volunteer or paid, should be supervised to ensure quality and safety. Religious organizations are the same as any other business and are obligated to provide proof their staff is competent to work with kids.

Use good judgment.

Parents need to exercise good judgment. Letting children wander alone to the bathroom or to get a drink isn't recommended, even if they are in church.

Allowing children to go on church trips with people whom parents do not know is not a good idea. People tend to see what they want to see. Parents may trust too much when trust isn't warranted or deny abuse because they don't want to believe it could be true.

Identify if the community is appropriately welcoming and friendly.

If so, this may be a sign of a well-adjusted congregation. When people are aloof or suspicious, these are indications that it may not be a comfortable place for you or your child. Beware of communities and individuals that seem too friendly. While that may sound like a contradiction, people who have ill intentions toward children have been found to overactively cultivate relationships with children and families in order to gain trust and access to kids. The key is that adult behavior must be appropriate and balanced.

Watch how people interact with children.

People who work with children need to know how to talk and work with kids. Ministers, education directors, and teachers are particularly important. Observe how religious leaders interact with children and how children respond to them. Are children free to speak their mind or are they nervous to say what they think? Visit religious instruction classrooms or volunteer to help on church trips; it's a quick and easy way to determine if children are treated respectfully. Negligence is the most common cause for harm, so avoid adults who seem preoccupied or inattentive. Adults who promote themselves too much may be trying to set up dependency or an abusive situation. Traits of abusive clergy include excessive power, control-oriented leadership, spiritual elitism, manipulation of members, perceived persecution, lifestyle rigidity, emphasis on experience, suppression of dissent, harsh discipline, and denunciation of others whose ideologies conflict with their own.

Is a child abuse policy present?

Does the religious organization have a child abuse prevention policy in place? If so, what does it say? Some define abuse as something a child may experience in their home but have no mention of it occurring within church walls or jurisdiction. Good child abuse policies have considered potential risks and problems and put into place a plan to avoid problems. The Louisville *Courier-Journal* found that five times fewer children were abused in religious organizations after policies were created. Good policies protect children.

Is the religious organization insured?

Insurance agencies have identified that religious organizations could be at risk of being sued if children are abused while in their care. Religious bodies that don't have a child abuse prevention program may not be eligible for insurance. Organizations such as the Nonprofit Risk Management Center, Church Mutual Insurance Company, and the Church Law and Tax Report are good resources to help churches develop guidelines for child protection, especially in the areas of clergy misconduct and child sexual abuse.

Types of programs.

All religious organizations have created programs to educate and inspire youngsters, and it is up to the parents to determine if they approve of the messages being conveyed, as well as their delivery. Most religious organizations have an educational curriculum that is used, which will give parents some guidelines of what to expect. Talking with those who will be in charge of the program will help parents know if their children's needs will be addressed.

Identify if a record of past allegations exists.

Accidents can happen within any institution, and the way that the organization handles incidents can be instructive. Find out what kinds of child maltreatment problems have occurred in the past and how those problems were handled. When allegations are made, organizations should keep detailed, accurate, and thorough records, and reports should be made to child protective organizations. Even events that seem small should be noted, because they may be an indication of bigger problems.

Are escorts and monitors present?

Because religious organizations have an open admittance policy, children are better protected when established members sit with newcomers or are present to intervene when adults act inappropriately or suspiciously around children.

Is there an open door policy?

The physical structure of religious buildings may be conducive to preventing or promoting abuse. Clergy may close doors in order to keep the noise down and conversations private, but doors should be kept open so children can be seen by others. When there are no other people around beside the child and adult, it puts children at risk. Boys are at just as much risk of being sexually abused as girls.

Volunteer policies.

The presence or absence of volunteer policies gives parents a good idea about the institution's commitment to child safety. It is recommended that all volunteers working with children and youth be active members of the congregation for at least six months. New members are encouraged to participate in volunteer opportunities, such as serving as greeters and participating in choir, which help people to get to know them, but not engage in services that put children directly at risk. All volunteers who work with children, youth, or vulnerable adults should complete a volunteer form, be given a job description detailing their responsibilities and undergo training. Volunteers under the age of eighteen should always be supervised. Obviously, volunteers convicted of abuse should not have contact with children.

Gifts, threats, and bribes.

Children may be threatened or bribed in order to gain their compliance. Money, gifts, alcohol, good grades, scholarships, spiritual opportunities, and recreational activities have all been used to discourage youth from divulging clergy improprieties. As example, sexual abuse victim Ron Snipp described Rev. Arthur Wood as a surrogate father who taught him to drive; took him to circuses, rodeos, and vacations; and encouraged him to go into the priesthood. If a child disproportionately receives things that others don't, it is appropriate to wonder why.

Consider size of the religious community.

The size of a congregation influences the types of risks involved. Small congregations may have more of a family feel to them. When everyone knows everyone else, people who pose potential risk can be avoided. But sometimes, when people are comfortable with each other, they can be too trusting and are willing to overlook potential problems. In larger religious organizations, there are more eyes around to observe wrongdoing and, as a result, potential abuse may be reduced. Larger organizations may have more formalized rules, principles, and guidelines, and they may have developed a broader safety net for their students. On the other hand, it is difficult to really know all of the members in large organizations and hard to know details of people's pasts.

There are more places for potential abuse to occur and more fluctuations in member traffic. In large institutions, people may erroneously assume that someone else is monitoring caregivers.

Is the organization open to change for kids?

It is possible that religious congregations that don't have safeguards in place need help to establish policies and guidelines to protect the children, staff, and community. Offering to serve on committees to help develop child protection strategies can be useful to both parents and organizations. Once the congregation has decided to create policies to protect children, the National Committee for Prevention of Child Abuse encourages the development of a child safety plan, which includes things like applications for all workers and volunteers, annual training for staff and volunteers who work with children, and protocols for how to handle allegations of abuse.

PROMISING PROGRAMS

Some faiths and denominations have actively developed policies and materials to help local religious communities create child abuse prevention programs. Religious organizations such as the Rabbinical Assembly, United Methodist Church, Women of Reformed Judaism, and United Church of Christ have formed national advisory committees to address how religious communities have responded to child maltreatment by clergy. Denominations that have created child safety resolutions include the National Council of Churches, Christian Church (Disciples of Christ), Evangelical Lutheran Church in America, Presbyterian Church, Seventh-Day Adventists, United Church of Christ, Evangelical Lutheran Church, and the United Methodist Church. The National Council of Churches offers a "bibliography of resources for the religious community" called the Child Abuse Ministry. It includes resources for congregations and clergy, for children and youth, for parents, for adult survivors, and curriculum and video resources and resource organizations. The National Conference of Catholic Bishops has created the Walk in the Light program to encourage appropriate pastoral response to child sexual abuse. The Episcopal Church has created the Children's Charter for the Church and has many resources on preventing child abuse. The Presbyterian Church and the Church of Jesus Christ of Latter-day Saints have taken firm positions against the abuse of children. The United Methodist Church has developed publications on how to select and screen church workers, the Orthodox Church in America has created a resource on youth safety and liability issues, and the United Pentecostal Church International has addressed the issue of legal liability in child abuse in the church and stated, "The well-being of our children and young people is the primary reason for implementing protective measures.... Prevention is the only real solution." A comprehensive child protection packet published by the Unitarian Universalist Association of Congregations includes: an ethical statement on safety and proper relations in the congregations, a sermon by a child abuse minister, a healing service for abuse survivors and congregations, samples of safety policies and volunteer contracts, information on reporting procedures, and a resource list of prevention programs and resources. Jehovah's Witnesses are concerned about safeguarding children from harm and promote prevention through their publications. The policy statement of Old Emanuel Lutheran Church of Inver Grove Heights, Minnesota, leaves no doubt of its official position:

> It is the determination of the church to provide a Christian
> environment that is safe, both for those receiving its ministries and for
> those providing its ministries. Sexual abuse, sexual exploitation,
> sexual harassment and physical abuse is not tolerated. If those
> employees or volunteers who provide the ministries of the church
> should engage in these behaviors they would violate the terms of their
> employment or voluntary service. A violation of this guideline could
> result in disciplinary action, termination of employment or dismissal.

Many churches have constructed child protection policies that recognize child abuse and neglect as serious problems that can damage people's perception of and trust in God, devastate families, and divide congregations. As a result, some, like the Lutheran Church, have worked to provide and care for children in a safe environment by establishing procedures to protect children from abuse and neglect.

Child abuse is ecumenical. It can occur within any religious organization or faith. When clear policies and strict penalties are established by religious organizations to deal with the problem of child maltreatment, child abuse is reduced. While prevention strategies are frequently created as a result of organizational self-preservation concerns, the fact that safeguards are in place is a positive step. Religious organizations have a wonderful opportunity to act as a role model for the community about how to safely care for the littlest sheep in the flock.

RESOURCES

American Bar Association
321 North Clark St.
Chicago, IL 60610
(312) 988-5000
http://www.abanet.org

Awareness Center
Jewish Coalition Against Sexual Abuse/
Assault
PO Box 65273
Baltimore, MD 21209
(443) 857-5560
http://theawarenesscenter.org

Children's Defense Fund
25 E Street, NW
Washington, DC 20001
(202) 628-8787
(800) CDF-1200 (800-233-1200)
http://www.childrensdefense.org

Church Mutual Insurance Company
PO Box 357
3000 Schuster Lane
Merrill, WI 54452-0357
(800) 554-2642 and (715) 536-5577
http://www.churchmutual.com

Church Law and Tax Report
PO Box 2600
Big Sandy, TX 75755
http://www.churchlawtoday.com/cltr
info.php

Nonprofit Risk Management Center
1130 Seventeenth Street, NW, Suite 210
Washington, DC 20036
(202) 785-3891
www.nonprofitriskmanagement.com

Survivors First
PO Box 81-172
Wellesley Hills, MA 02481
(781) 910-5467
http://bbs.survivorsfirst.org

Survivors Network of those Abused by
Priests (SNAP)
PO Box 6416
Chicago, IL 60680-6416
(877) 762-7432
www.snapnetwork.org

Voice of the Faithful
PO Box 1007
N. Esconset, NY 11767
(631) 979-0476
www.votf.org

REFERENCES

Advocate Times. "Clergy Abuse." 2004.
http://alterboys.tripod.com/Faith/
Clergy_Abuse_x.html.

Anderson, Jeffrey. "Vatican Named a
Defendant in Clergy Sex Abuse
Lawsuits." *National Catholic
Reporter.* (19 April 2002): 1.

Associated Press. "Pa. Pastor Arrested in Endangerment." 11 January 1999. http://www.nospank.net/n-d95.htm.

Awareness Center. "Rabbinical Abuse." 2006. http://theawarenesscenter.org/lanner_baruch.html.

Beal, John P. "Doing What One Can Do: Canon Law and Clerical Sexual Misconduct." *The Jurist* 52, no. 2 (1992): 642–683.

Belluck, Pam. "New Documents Show Church Knew of Concern about Priest." *New York Times,* 26 April 2002, A18.

Berry, Jason, and Andrew Greeley. *Lead Us Not into Temptation: Catholic Priests and the Sexual Abuse of Children.* Urbana: University of Illinois Press, 2000.

"Bishop Accountability." http://www.bishop-accountability.org/resources/resource-files/databases/BaltimorePriests.htm.

Boston Globe, "Clergy Sex Abuse." 2004. http://www.boston.com/globe/abuse stories.

Brincefield, James. "Clergy Malpractice." *Moving Forward* 2, no. 4 (2004): 9.

Carroll, Matt. "Suspended Priest Was Accused Earlier." *Boston Globe,* 20 March 2002, A30.

———. *Betrayal: The Crisis in the Catholic Church.* Hinckley, Ill.: Little, Brown, 2004.

CBS News. "The Church on Trial." http://www.cbsnews.com/stories/2002/06/11/60II/main511845.shtml.

Center for the Prevention of Sexual and Domestic Violence in Seattle. "Sexual Violence." http://www.ncdsv.org/publications_domviolence.html.

Christian Church—Disciples of Christ. http://www.disciples.org.

Church of Jesus Christ of Latter-day Saints. http://www.lds.org.

Cimbolic, Peter. "The Identification and Treatment of Sexual Disorders and the Priesthood." *Jurist* 52, no. 2 (1992): 598–614.

Clines, Francis. "Nearly 100 Kentucky Men Add to Accusations Against Priests." *New York Times,* 28 May 2002, A15.

Cobble, James, and Richard Hammer. "Selecting and Screening Church Workers." *Christian Ministry Resources.* Matthew, N.C., 1996.

Cooperman, Alan. "Two Families Seek Church Accountability in Abuse Cases." www.fairness.com/resources/relation?relation_id=8637&offset.

Courier-Journal (Louisville, Ky.) "Newspaper Review of Church Abuse Suits Shows Patterns." 29 September 2002. http://www.rickross.com/reference/clergy/clergy103.html.

Crary, David. "For Victims of Abuse by Clergy, the Common Bond Is Feeling of Broken Trust." Survivors Network of those Abused by Priests. http://www.snapnetwork.org/psych_effects/victims_common_bond.htm.

Cullen, Kevin. "A 31-Year-Old Case Focuses

Ireland on Child Abuse, Neglect."
Boston Globe, 9 May 2002, A1.

Davis, Michael. "The Shanley Case."
Boston Globe. 2004. http://
www.boston.com/globe/spotlight/
abuse/shanley.

Demarest, Sylvia. "Father Figure." *Metro.*
http://www.metroactive.com/
papers/metro/06.27.02/priests-
0226.html.

Enroth, Ronald M. *Churches That Abuse.*
Grand Rapids, Mich.: Zondervan
Publishing House, 1992.

Episcopal Church. http://www.episcopal
church.org.

Farragher, Thomas. "Church Cloaked in
Culture of Silence." *Boston Globe,* 24
February 2002, A1.

———. "John Geoghan: Abuse, Inmate,
Victim." 2005. http://
http://www.boston.com/news/
specials/geoghan.

Firestone, David. "Child Abuse at a
Church Creates a Stir in Atlanta." *New
York Times,* 30 March 2001, A13.

Friday, Carolyn. "Priests and Abuse."
Newsweek (16 August 1993): 122, no 7,
42–45.

Gaskell, Stephanie. "NY Priest Placed on
Leave in 1997 Assigned to Parish."
Boston Globe, 20 March 2002: A30.

Goode, Erica. "Abusive Priests Are Varied,
but Treatable, Center Found." *New
York Times,* 26 April 2002, A19.

Haywood, T. "Cycle of Abuse and
Psychopathology in Cleric and
Noncleric Molesters of Children and
Adolescents." *Child Abuse and Neglect*
20, vol. 12 (1999): 1233–1243.

Jehovah's Witnesses. http://
www.watchtower.org.

Jenkins, P. "Accusations of Abuse are Anti-
Catholic Propaganda." In *Child Abuse:
Opposing Viewpoints,* edited by Katie
de Koster and Karen Swisher. San
Diego, Calif.: Greenhaven Press, 1994:
167–175.

Kelly, Matt. "Catholic Sex Abuse Case
Widens in Military." Survivors
Network of Those Abused by Priests.
http://www.snapnetwork.org/news/
otherstates/scandal_in_military.htm.

Lewis, Raphael, and Jamal Watson. "Worst
Fears: Abuse Case Baffles Town,
Parish." *Boston Globe,* 18 June 2000, B1.

Lutheran Church. http://www.lca.org.

Matchan, Linda. "Thank God You Didn't
Have to Live With Him." *Boston Globe,*
5 June 2002, D1.

Murphy, Dean. "For 2 Decades in 3
Countries, Priest Left a Trail of Sex
Abuse." *New York Times,* 20 April
2002, A1.

National Conference of Catholic Bishops.
http://www.usccb.org.

National Council of Churches.
http://www.ncccusa.org.

Newton, Michael. "Denial." Court TV
Crime Library. http://
www.crimelibrary.com/serial_killers/
predators/porter/index_1.html.

Nikolai, Geri. "Appeal Set in Priest's
Abuse Case: Diocesan Officials Are
Held in Contempt For Not Giving Up

Personnel Data About Mark Campobello." *Rockford Register Star,* 23 May 2003.

Nonprofit Risk Management Center. "Screening of Employees." http://www.nonprofitriskmanagement.com.

Old Emanuel Lutheran Church. http://www.worshiphere.org/MN/InverGroveHeights.htm.

Orthodox Church in America. http://www.oca.org.

Paulson, Michael. "Dorchester Parish Struggles to Survive." *Boston Globe.* http://www.boston.com/globe/spotlight/abuse/stories5/010404_parish 1993.

————. "Results of Session Disappoint Some." *Boston Globe,* 25 April 2002, A1.

Pfeiffer, Sacha. "Priest Pleads Guilty to Raping Altar Boy." *Boston Globe.* http://www.boston.com/globe/spotlight/abuse/extras/paquin_archive.htm.

Presbyterian Church. http://www.pcusa.org.

Protection of the Theotokos. "Metropolitan Pangratios Vrionis." http://www.pokrov.org/Abusers/pvrionis.html.

Rabbinical Assembly. http://www.rabbinicalassembly.org.

Ramsland, Katherine. "David Koresch." *Crime Library.* http://www.crimelibrary..com/notorious_murders/not_guilty/koresh/1.html.

Rick A. Ross Institute for the Study of Destructive Cults, Controversial Groups and Movements. "Clergy abuse." http://www.rickross.com/groups/clergy.html.

Ripley, Amanda. "Father Paul Shanley Didn't Hide His Interest in Pedophilia So Why Didn't the Church Recognize Him as a Problem?" *Time Magazine* (22 April 2002): 47.

Robinson, Walter, and Sacha Pfeiffer. "Court Records Show Priest Abuse Hidden." *Boston Globe,* 16 February 2002, A1.

Rosenblatt, Gary. "Stolen Innocence." *The Jewish Week,* 30 January 2003 http://www.thejewishweek.com/news/newscontent.php3?artid=3817.

Rubino, Stephen. "Suffer the Parents: Clergy Sexual Abuse of Children." *Trial* 32 (18–22 September 1996).

Seventh-day Adventists. http://www.adventist.org.

Smith, Peter. "Jefferson Man Says Priest Abused Him." *Courtroom Law,* 19 April 2002. http://www.courtroomlaw.com/catholic_case.shtml.

South Eastern Center Against Sexual Assault. "Effects of Clergy Abuse." http://www.secasa.com.au/index.php/survivors/51/165/4.

Survivors Network of Those Abused by Priests. "Psychological Effects of Sexual Abuse." 2005. http://www.snapnetwork.org/psych_effects/effectsindex.htm on kids.

Sullivan, Andrew. "They Know Not What They Do." *Time* (6 May 2002): 31.

Swanson, Doug J. "Church Abuse Focus of Database: Dallas Lawyer Completes National List of 2,600 'Priest Perpetrators'." *Dallas Morning News*, 30 October 2004. http://bishop_account ability.org/about_us/2004_10_30_ Swanson_ChurchAbuse.htm.

Unitarian Universalist Association. http://www.uua.org.

United Church of Christ. http://www.ucc. org.

United Methodist Church. http://www. umc.org.

United Pentecostal Church International. http://www.ucpi.org.

Vincent, Lynn. "Breaking Faith." http:// www.leaderu.com/theology/ breakingfaith.html.

Wakin, Daniel. "When Priests Were Accused, Quest for Secrecy Followed." *New York Times*, 12 March 2002. A1.

Wikipedia. "Jim Jones." http://en. wikipedia.org/wiki/Jim_Jones.

———. "Roman Catholic Sex Abuse Scandal." http://en.wikipedia.org/ wiki/Roman_Catholic_Church_sex_ abuse_scandal.

Wilgoren, Jodi. "First Casualties of the One-Sin-You're-Out Policy." *New York Times*, 17 June 2002, A1.

Women of Reform Judaism. http://wrj.rj. org.

Worldwide Faith News. "ELCA Settles Texas Civil Case With 14 Plaintiff." http://www.wfn.org/2004/04/msg 00082.html.

Wypijewski, Joanne. "The Passion of Father Paul Shanley." *Legal Affairs*. http://www.legalaffairs.org/issues/ September–October–2004/feature_ wypijewski_sepocto4.msp.

Yardley, Jim. "Abuse By Clergy Is Not Just a Catholic Problem." *New York Times*, 13 April 2002, A13. 2002.

York, Dwight. "Court Upholds Conviction of Nubian Leader." http://www. firstcoastnews.com/news/georgia/ news-article.aspx?storyid=46342.

Chapter 6 "On My Honor" Abuse in Scouts and Civic Organizations

The local Boy Scout troop asked my church's Mission Board for permission to use the building for meetings. As a board member, I had mixed feelings about its request. My mother had been a Scout leader, and my brother and cousins had been Scouts. However, another family member had been sexually abused when he was at Boy Scout camp; additionally, I knew that a Scout leader's son in my town had sold his father's pornographic magazines to other boys on the elementary school playground at recess. These experiences made me question the assumption that all Scout leaders are good role models. The board knew it must make a careful and reasoned decision. Discussion quickly revealed that none of us knew the current Scout leader or his assistants, we had no idea about what they would actually be doing while on church premises, and we knew there would be no church representatives present to oversee their activities. Many children in the community, from ages six to eighteen, would attend functions each week. The Boy Scouts would pay nothing for the use of the space, they didn't have their own insurance, and leaders wanted keys to the building so they could come and go as they pleased. The board realized that if a child was injured or molested on church grounds, the church could be sued. While the minister, as leader of the church, might be targeted in a lawsuit, we, the committee who authorized the use of the space by this organization, felt we would ultimately be responsible. After a lively debate, the committee denied the Boy Scouts use of the church, because safeguards were not in place to protect both children and the church. The Scout leaders had not taken appropriate precautions to make sure that children from the community would be safe. The committee took the position that it didn't matter what the reputation of the organization was—every group should be held accountable to the same standards of proving safety to children.

Children may participate in a variety of groups that promote service to others, teach job or recreational skills, or encourage character development by disseminating patriotic, religious, or ideological values. Just a few possible organizations include Scouts, Civil Air Patrol, Junior Achievement, Odyssey of the Mind, Young Democrats or Young Republicans, Boys & Girls Clubs, Camp Fire Girls and Boys, YMCA, Big Brothers Big Sisters, 4-H, Students Against Drunk Driving, Children of the Confederacy, DeMolay, Rainbow Girls, and hobby groups like Teen Association of Model Railroaders. Kids may join theater companies, bands, choruses, or other artistic groups for similar reasons. Children's participation in these groups can be a wonderful way for them to learn important skills and values from other adults while gaining reinforcement and support from a peer network. Most of these groups have an open-admission policy for both children and the adults who act as their leaders. The American Bar Association estimates that eighty-eight million children attend civic or recreational groups each year, which puts them in contact with fifteen million employees or volunteers. These programs provide an important safety net for children who need adult supervision and guidance. Many, such as the Boy Scouts and Girl Scouts or Big Brothers Big Sisters of America, have developed extensive programs and policies to promote youth safety. But the best-intended programs are only as effective as the individuals who run them. While most children are safer by participating in these organizations than they would be alone and unsupervised, some do get hurt, mistreated, or abused. But how many? That is unknown. Are media allegations of impropriety in such organizations accurate or sensationalized? Let us turn now to some of the major groups that have generated recent concern regarding children's safety.

Scouting.

Scouting is the most well-known civic youth organization worldwide. Juliette Lowe founded the Girl Scouts around a century ago, around the same time that the Boy Scouts were founded by Lord Robert Baden Powell in England. Both the Boy Scouts and Girl Scouts have national policies designed to put safe, responsible volunteers in charge of children, but these practices are not always implemented at the local level. Both types of Scouts have been responsible in attempting to reduce risk among leaders, with around twenty thousand volunteer criminal background checks being conducted each month. While reference checks are supposed to occur before adults assume leadership roles, there is usually no probationary period and no education requirement. Training is provided by former Scouts; expertise in child development or administrative leadership is desirable but not necessary. The extent of background checks and the degree of training varies by troop and region.

While the Boy Scouts and Girl Scouts both have formal policies to discourage child maltreatment, they each seem to address the issue of risk differently.

Boy Scouts of America. The Boy Scouts of America (BSA) promotes the development of skills, appreciation of the outdoors, community service, good citizenship, and religious values. The Boy Scout law encourages boys to be trustworthy, loyal, helpful, friendly, courteous, kind, obedient, cheerful, thrifty, brave, clean, and reverent. Scouting in other countries may have a similar foundation but may not adhere to all of the values endorsed by the BSA, such as emphasis on heterosexuality. The Boy Scouts have developed programs to reduce unacceptable social problems such as hunger, illiteracy, unemployment, drug abuse, and child abuse. Famous former Scouts include President John F. Kennedy, actors Henry Fonda and Jimmy Stewart, baseball player Hank Aaron, as well as astronauts Neil Armstrong and John Glenn.

Data indicates that, despite the values encouraged through scouting, Boy Scouts may not always be safe when in the care of their leaders. Scouts have been injured and even died at camp activities, national jamborees, and campouts. Many have run into problems on hikes and outdoor adventures when exposed to bad weather or the poor judgment of Scout leaders. But perhaps the biggest safety concern surrounds the issue of sexual abuse. Over 1,151 boys reported being sexually abused by Boy Scout leaders over the twenty years prior to 1991 when author Patrick Boyle disclosed that sexual abuse is commonplace in the BSA, which he refers to as "a magnet for pedophiles." Boyle found that abuse exists throughout the entire organization, from the national level to local troops. Former Eagle Scout Douglas Smith was the national director of the BSA's programs at its headquarters in Texas for thirty-nine years when he suddenly retired. Months later, he was sentenced for the possession and trafficking of child pornography after hundreds of sexually explicit images of boys were found on his computer. Ironically, in his position as program director for the Boy Scouts of America, Smith was in charge of writing rules to prevent Boy Scouts from being sexually abused.

The BSA discharged 1,800 scoutmasters who were suspected of molesting boys between 1971 and 1991, an average of 90 a year. The BSA reports 100 new cases of child sexual abuse a year and maintains 2,000 child maltreatment cases on file at any time. The official figures are probably lower than what actually occurs, because most boys do not disclose their abuse. Boys in all fifty states have reported being sexually abused by their scout leaders, from a Chicago Cub Scout leader who was sentenced to ninety years for sexually abusing four boys in attacks that left three of them infected with venereal disease to a Somerville, Massachusetts, troop leader who pleaded guilty to child rape and abuse that lasted more than five years and included boys being blindfolded and handcuffed to a bed. Sexual molestation has most frequently occurred while boys were at remote camps with no one around who could protect them but has also occurred on field trips and at the homes of leaders.

The Boy Scouts' leadership actively sought to prevent child sexual abuse beginning in the 1980s. They hired consultants to design abuse prevention and control programs. They created videotapes such as *It Happened to Me* and *A Time to Tell*, which encourage Scouts to recognize, resist, and report sexual abuse. They have developed online protection training, and their child abuse prevention materials are widely used by a variety of churches and organizations. Their abuse prevention emphasis ranges from safety to acquaintance rape, Internet safety, and stalking.

Despite their prevention efforts, abuse has occurred. The BSA headquarters reports there are about 68 child molesters out of 150,000 leaders yearly. It is estimated that there are 1.5 million leaders and volunteers working with over three million boys. In this respect, the number of abuses may actually be quite small.

But analysts such as Patrick Boyle allege that the BSA has dragged its feet by not aggressively addressing abuse allegations. In 1984, the BSA paid two million dollars just for insurance premiums. According to a study of fifty lawsuits against it, it has paid over fifteen million dollars since 1986 to settle lawsuits from boys who were sexually abused by Scout leaders. The BSA's values are designed to promote belief in a supreme being, which does discriminate against boys who are atheists or who don't profess to be religious. They also reinforce a heterosexual lifestyle, and leaders are not supposed to be homosexual. Every organization adheres to its own values, policies, and practices. Parents need to realize this and assess whether its philosophy is right for their sons and if their sons have characteristics that make them subject to alienation, expulsion, or abuse.

Girl Scouts. The Girls Scouts regards itself as an entirely different organization from the Boy Scouts, even though it too has scouting programs for youngsters and older teens. The Girl Scouts has not faced the kinds of abuse allegations as the Boy Scouts. It credits this to a difference in organizational structure: the Girl Scouts has established a set of procedures and practices to protect girls in a "two-deep" policy of leadership that requires two trained adults to be present with the girls at all times. This policy has reduced actual abuse as well as accusations of impropriety. The Girl Scouts, like the Boy Scouts, has developed a series of publications that pertain to safety and risk management issues. The Girl Scout manual, SafetyWise, provides a list of child-abuse prevention guidelines, but like the Boy Scouts, its safeguards are only as good as the adults who implement them. For instance, a recommended ratio of adults to girls exists, but this recommendation can be ignored if volunteers are limited. SafetyWise states that any lifeguard at Scout-sponsored activities must be over the age of eighteen, but it can be a person under the age of sixteen depending upon the laws in each state. While many states require that a certified water safety instructor be present for all swimming activities, some leaders break this rule to give Scouts the opportunity to swim if their parents sign waivers.

Girl Scouts have been given the charge of pursuing independence within the umbrella of their organizational mandate. While all troops use the same core materials, each chooses its own program emphasis. For instance, the Lone Star Girl Scout Council in Austin, Texas, follows the National Girl Scout Association's theme of developing self-potential, relating to others, developing values, and contributing to society. The Abenaki Girl Scout Council in Brewer, Maine places stronger emphases on leading girls to math, science, technology, cultural diversity and environmental concern while developing leadership and self-esteem. Just as programs can vary considerably, so does the leadership. While the national organization has set policies and a tone for the organization as a whole, the manuals clearly state that it is the responsibility of the local Girl Scout Council to ensure the health, safety, and well-being of girls. Scout leaders are supposed to take training courses and have certification to prove they're safe and reliable; for instance, one adult volunteer from each troop is required to have an outdoor training certificate to take girls hiking or camping and basic Red Cross first aid training. When interviewed, some Scout leaders indicated that they had not taken the proper training courses but were approved to work with large numbers of girls merely by claiming that they were experienced. These included a 120-girl camp director who had never taken the training program or run a camp and a leader who took 26 girls hiking for days at a time who had never taken the outdoor training class. Because of these implementation problems, the national association has created strict procedures for the qualifications of adults who work with the girls.

Research indicates that the Girls Scouts has not had the problem of sexual abuse allegations that the Boy Scouts has experienced. When sexual abuse allegations were made in the Girl Scouts, they appeared to be girl-to-girl, not leader-to-boy contact, as in the Boy Scouts. Child sexual abuse tends to be a male-dominated perpetrator activity, and most Girl Scout leaders are females. Nurturing behavior is regarded as more natural for women, which may also explain why women have not been targeted as perpetrators. Overnight programs can provide kids with opportunity for sexual contact, so the Girl Scouts has found it necessary to train leaders on how to prevent camper-to-camper sexual contact. To avoid abuse, the Girl Scouts has also dramatically altered their cookie sales program after realizing that door-to-door sales posed potential danger for the girls.

Therefore, both Girl Scouts and Boy Scouts provide important messages and opportunities for youth to learn and serve. The biggest difference between them when it comes to child safety appears to be structural: organizationally, the Girl Scouts appears to have been more proactive regarding issues of child safety, while the Boy Scouts has been more reactive. The BSA is taking steps to rectify the problem. Parents must realize that when their child belongs to an international organization such as the Scouts, there is great variation in leadership and activities from place to place; it is their job to investigate and make sure their local Scout troop provides what they and their child need.

Big Brothers Big Sisters.

For almost a century, Big Brothers Big Sisters of America has served over a million children through one-to-one relationships between adult volunteers and children at risk. The volunteers act as mentors and role models to help youth increase their self-confidence and reach their highest potential. More than five hundred Big Brothers Big Sisters agencies nationwide match adult volunteers with children based on the child's specific needs and common interests. A recent study conducted by Public/Private Ventures in Philadelphia found that this program had a positive impact on children. Little Brothers and Sisters who met with their adult volunteers were 46 percent less likely to start using drugs, 27 percent less likely to start using alcohol, 52 percent less likely to skip school, and 33 percent less likely to hit someone; they were also more trusting of their parents, less likely to lie, and felt more supported in general. While the stereotype is that children in this type of program are deprived of at least one parent figure and are starving for attention, about a third of the children in this program come from two-parent homes. They are regarded as good kids whose parents recognized that they could benefit from some extra support.

Nationally, Big Brothers Big Sisters has created a standardized, comprehensive volunteer screening process that all affiliated agencies must follow. All applicants must have background checks, criminal and driving records, six references, and personal interviews. Use of the Child Abuse Potential (CAP) Inventory to screen volunteers for Big Brothers Big Sisters was found to discriminate between volunteers who agency staff rated excellent versus those rated bad. Yet in a study of male child abuse perpetrators who were given the CAP, only half of the offenders scored in the dangerous realm, indicating that while tests like the CAP can be helpful, they should be only part of a screening process. The reality is that even comprehensive screening processes cannot completely ensure the safety of children. Big Brothers Big Sisters should know. Some of its screened volunteers have been arrested on charges of sexual assault of children. These include volunteers at Big Brothers Big Sisters in Colorado, Texas, Illinois, Michigan, and in Ohio, where a Big Brother was charged with twenty-four counts of rape of a boy he was mentoring. Organizations must make decisions about whether it is in the children's best interest to permit volunteers to work with them. This may be difficult when there are no hard facts to indicate they should not. Providing kids with no adult mentor at all may be a higher risk. Of the 20,000 New Hampshire children in need of an adult adviser or mentor, only 1,300 have found one. Demand for services is both a blessing and a curse for organizations: past successes make parents want to use these kinds of programs, but when demand exceeds supply, an organization must be careful not to take just anybody and thereby increase the risk of abuse and decrease the respect of the program. Dr. Bill Maier, a psychologist in residence with Focus on the Family, indicates that Big Brothers Big Sisters, like many voluntary organizations, does not have large enough volunteer applicant pools to meet the needs of every child; this is complicated when parents do not want certain kinds of people to serve as volunteers for their children. The national organization has a nondiscrimination policy that prohibits exclusion of potential volunteers, staff, youth, or parents on the basis of race, color, religion, national origin, gender, marital status, sexual orientation, veteran status, or disability, but parents still have the right to refuse any volunteer who does not seem to be a good fit for their child.

The leadership of Big Brothers Big Sisters has realized that its traditional one-on-one mentoring relationship does have a certain degree of risk. While it continues to accept the view that most people are good, it has beefed up its supervision program. The Boston program utilizes a customer service call center with mentors, children, and their parents. Good supervision and monitoring protects children.

YMCA.

The Young Men's Christian Association (YMCA) was founded in London in 1844 in response to unhealthy social conditions arising in the big cities during the Industrial Revolution. George Williams, a farm boy, came to London as a sales assistant in a department store. Appalled by streets filled with pickpockets, beggars, prostitutes, and abandoned children, he organized the first YMCA to substitute Bible study and prayer for life on the streets. His organization crossed the lines that separated all the different churches and social classes in England. Its idea caught on, and it is now a worldwide organization that serves millions of children through hundreds of different activities. The most enduring is its camp program. Day camp for children, provided by 1,537 YMCAs is the most widely offered program nationwide, and teen versions are offered at 770 locations. Sleep-away camps vary from general all-purpose camps to those that offer environmental education, arts, sports, or academics. In recent years, the YMCA movement has emphasized four core values—caring, honesty, respect, and responsibility—which it incorporates into all of its programs. It hopes to help youth to engage in pro-social, healthy behaviors and reduce antisocial, unhealthy, risky ones.

The YMCA serves over nine million kids in more than 2,400 facilities nationwide. It has well-defined programs and strict guidelines about who can care for young children. A medical advisory committee guides the YMCA, especially regarding physical safety issues in facilities. Efforts are made to prevent staff or volunteers from being alone with children. Despite prevention efforts, their national office reports that there are a few accusations of child maltreatment received each year. While most accusations focus on staff or volunteer abuse, allegations of member–on-member attack have also surfaced. Littleton, Colorado's YMCA was ordered to pay $375,000 in damages for allowing conditions in which a teenager sexually abused boys on its premises. Most abuse allegations have not been as serious as the abuse inflicted by Danvers, Massachusetts, YMCA staff member Christopher Reardon. A counselor and swimming instructor for the YMCA, Reardon confessed to seventy-five sexual abuse and molestation charges after investigators found pornographic videos and more than 2,000 diary entries of abusive behavior with three hundred boys, complete with detailed descriptions of their genitalia and how he had molested them. Reardon seemed like a safe bet because he was good with kids, actively involved in church youth programs, and, like many pedophiles, was involved in all the things where kids were, but he engaged in what lawyers called a pattern of premeditated, sexually predatory behavior toward preadolescent boys.

OTHER TYPES OF GROUPS

There are many other organizations and civic groups that children can belong to, and all of them should have safeguards in place to avoid the abuse of children. Parents are advised to inquire if the organization has implemented abuse precautions, and they should get to know individual leaders to determine if they approve of how they will interact with their children. Just a few such groups include:

Ideological groups.

Organizations with distinct ideological views may target youth as potential recruits. Most children and youth want to make the world a better place and leaders can use that enthusiasm for good or to perpetuate their own ideological position. Such groups incorporate young recruits into activities in hopes they will become active adult members. Some of these groups are strictly political, such as Young Republicans or Young Democrats, or they may have political causes attached, such as Junior ROTC or People for the Ethical Treatment of Animals (PETA). Other groups may have a religious orientation, such as Campus Crusade for Christ or Rainbow Girls. White supremacy groups recruit youth, as do groups that seek to promote their own racial, religious, ethnic, or nationalistic identity.

Community arts groups.

Art, music, dance, and theater programs are no longer necessarily part of the school curriculum because of funding cuts, but they provide children with important opportunities for self-expression. Participants may spend long hours together, travel to events, and be heavily influenced by a small number of adult leaders. Most groups value assistance, which helps parents keep an eye on the activities.

Hobby organizations.

Children may become interested in trains, juggling, model aircraft, doll houses, or other hobbies and want to network with others who can help them to pursue their interests. This can be useful and productive, however, hobby organizations are also "anyone can come who is interested" groups, which means that parents have little control over who their children may meet. Attending the hobby meetings with the children, even if it means reading a book in the corner, may help parents to know that their kids are being exposed to good influences.

HOW TO CHOOSE A SAFE GROUP FOR YOUR CHILD

Civic and community groups can provide wonderful role modeling and experiences for children, but parents must know the people with whom their children interact in order to determine if they will be safe. Often we trust these organizations because they do good things; therefore, parents assume that the people who operate them must be good, too. This is not necessarily the case. If parents look critically at the different groups in a community, they will increase the chance that their children will be safe.

What is the organization's reputation?

Is it an established group with multiple subsidiaries and a clear mission and organizational structure? Is it a newer organization that few people seem to know much about? Is it a group that everyone you know seems to have their children in, or is an organization with mixed reviews? The Better Business Bureau or police department may be able to provide parents with some insight about unfamiliar groups. Parents often allow their kids to participate based on the organization's national reputation without detailed knowledge about the local group. While national reputation and organizational philosophy are important, so is the reputation of the local branch. Patterns vary tremendously both between and within organizations.

Find out if background checks have been done—or do your own.

Screening adults who work with kids helps keep children safe. When use of volunteers is essential for groups to exist, groups may take the best they can get, which sometimes means they're not the best people to work with kids. Even organizations that are run primarily by volunteers are subject to the same rules for safety as an organization that pays their employees. Usually volunteer checks are less stringent, because organizations don't want to turn off people willing to help. The principle of reasonable care in hiring applies to the selection of volunteers, who should be held to high standards.

Are there clear guidelines for leaders?

National organizations such as the Boy Scouts, Girl Scouts, YMCA, 4-H, and Boys & Girls Clubs of America have well-developed sets of guidelines for selecting and monitoring adult leaders. Parents can easily obtain this information to ascertain how well they address safety issues and determine how well are these guidelines are implemented. The quality of the staff can make the difference between a good and poor experience for kids.

Are the leaders too good to be true?

Former leaders in Boy Scouts and other community organizations who are arrested for child molestation teach us that pedophiles are often great with kids, which can make it difficult for their supervisors to suspect any inappropriate things they may do in private. It is often difficult for parents to discern between people with bad intentions posing as perfect providers and genuinely wonderful and well-intended providers. The best thing that parents can do is engage in ongoing monitoring of how the leaders interact with their children.

Are the activities appropriate?

Some activities are exciting but not safe, especially if they are not well-organized—for instance, taking children who are not strong hikers on winter hikes, inadequately dressed and without necessary emergency resources. Similarly, going whitewater rafting can be fun, but not for children who are weak swimmers. Catastrophes can unexpectedly occur unless risks are identified and anticipated. If an organization gives youth excess free time and allows unmonitored one-on-one interactions, there's the potential of risk. Just "hanging out" with other kids can be fun but children are better off with well-organized activities with a beneficial product. Knowing details of scheduled activities will help identify the degree of risk your kids face.

How do the organizations prevent abuse?

Every child-oriented organization should have a program or standards in place to keep all forms of abuse from occurring. No organization can risk the reputational, financial, and legal outcomes that result from abusive situations. If organizations don't have any position on abuse, find out why. Child-centered organizations may experience problems from time to time. What should be of concern to parents is how these organizations handle the problems. If they address them and establish preventive strategies, it is sign that children will likely be safe with them. But if they try to hide allegations or blame the child victims for adult misbehavior, this is a red flag of concern.

Find out who supervises or monitors the staff.

Civic organizations are harder to monitor than most child-centered organizations because they operate in more flexible ways. Many rely on volunteers or people who are not professionally trained to work with children. If there is no system to monitor what happens when children are engaged in activities, their parents must assume the task of supervision and monitoring.

Volunteer!

Parents will find that if they volunteer to help, their assistance will be gratefully received, and they will learn a lot about the organization's inner workings. Volunteering will enable parents to know more about the staff and activities, which should make them more comfortable about their children participating in programs when they're not around. Parents who volunteer are also better able to suggest organizational changes. According to the Carnegie Foundation, while 20,000 national and local youth organizations operate in the United States, many children aren't served because there aren't enough volunteers available to help. Parents who volunteer will be able to help other children while they're keeping an eye on their own. Besides, most children like when their parents are involved in their activities, as long as they don't help too much.

When parents assess how well organizations meet these criteria, they can send their children to them with increased confidence in their safety. There are, after all, many wonderful organizations and volunteers who can enrich children's lives, and it would be a shame to deprive children of these opportunities. The key is in how well organizations structure themselves to ensure that children are safe. Some do a great job, while others rely on trust and assume that everything will be fine without instituting proper safeguards to encourage that result.

PROMISING PROGRAMS

Many volunteer and community groups have a philanthropic focus and don't view themselves as businesses. This focus has insulated them from instituting safeguards, and it has also insulated them from rigorous parental scrutiny. Any organization that works with children, profit or nonprofit, must establish prevention protocols to protect children and themselves.

Businesses like the Nonprofit Risk Management Center provide assistance and resources for community-serving nonprofit organizations. It gives them practical, affordable suggestions for controlling risks that threaten an organization's ability to accomplish its mission. It also offers technical assistance, software, training, and consulting help on a vast array of risk management topics. It does not sell insurance or endorse organizations that do. As a business, it charges for its services and materials, but it can save an organization from future problems. The materials teach how to conduct interviews, check references, and manage staff and volunteers more effectively. Consultants will give practical ideas on how to avoid child abuse and insurance and transportation problems.

Organizations are advised to consider implementing recommended safeguards, and parents are advised to be familiar with what those recommended safeguards are and if the organizations their children want to join have implemented them. Problems occur within every organization, and the way that these organizations deal with them is a good indicator of how they'll address future improprieties. By creating safeguards, children, parents, and providers are all better protected.

RESOURCES

Big Brothers Big Sisters National Office
230 North 13th Street
Philadelphia, PA 19107
(215) 567-7000 (phone)
(215) 567-0394 (fax)
http://www.bbbsa.org

Boy Scouts of America National Council
PO Box 152079
Irving, TX 75015-2079
http://www.scouting.org

Camp Fire USA
1100 Walnut Street, Suite 1900
Kansas City, MO 64106-2197
(816) 285-2010
http://www.campfire.org

Girl Scouts of the USA
420 Fifth Avenue
New York, NY 10018-2798
(800) 478-7248 or (212) 852-8000
http://www.girlscouts.org

Nonprofit Risk Management Center
1130 Seventeenth Street, NW, Suite 210
Washington, DC 20036
(202) 785-3891
http://www.nonprofitriskmanagement.
com

Prevent Child Abuse America
500 N. Michigan Ave., # 200
Chicago, IL 60611
(312) 663-3520
http://www.preventchildabuse.org

YMCA of the USA
101 North Wacker Drive
Chicago, IL 60606
(800) 872-9622
http://www.ymca.net

First Nonprofit Companies
111 N. Canal Street, # 801
Chicago, IL 60606
(800) 520-4352
http://www.firstnonprofitcompanies.
com/

Risk Management Centers.
1520 2nd Street
Santa Monica, CA 90401
(888) 8-INJURY
http://www.eriskcenter.org/

Stay Safe
http://www.staysafe.info/newsletter_
05_2002

REFERENCES

Allison, Sue. "The Nuts and Bolts of
    Amusement Park Safety for This
    Summer's High Riders." *Life* 8 (August
    1985): 32.
Arave, Lynn. "Unsupervised Boy Scouts
    and Unsafe Conduct." *America's Roof.* -
    http://www.network54.com/Forum/
    3897/thread/1121379165/Kings+peak
    +report.
Associated Press. "Heat Exhaustion Adds
    to Scout Jamboree Woes: Leaders Who

Died May Have Ignored Safety Rules."
    http://www.msnbc.msn.com/id/
    8705262.
Barry, Ellen. "Troop Leaders Face Charges
    of Raping Scout." *Boston Globe*, 8 May
    1999, B1.
Boyle, Patrick. "Corporate Policy Kept Out
    Abuse." *Washington Times*, May 22,
    1991. http://www.newsline.umd.edu/
    Boyle/shonorsecret.htm.
Boyle, Peter. *Scouts Honor: Sexual Abuse*

in America's Most Trusted Institution.
Roclin, Calif.: Prima Publishing, 1994.

Boy Scouts of America. "Eliminating
Opportunities for Abuse." www.
scoutingvermont.org.

———. "Youth Protection and the Boy
Scouts of America. Detroit Area
Council." http://www.dacbsa.org/
YP/flyer-YouthProtectionandtheBSA
.pdf.

Cable News Network. "Ex-Scout Official
Sentenced for Child Porn." 5 December
2005. http://cnn.com. 12/5/2005.

Carbone, Ray. "On My Honor." *Foster's
Daily Democrat.* 26 March 2002, E1.

Channel 5 News. "'Big Brother of Year'
Sentenced to Prison for Molesting
Boy." http://www.newsnet5.com/
news/6616647/detail.html.

Contrador, Amy. "Why Isn't Sexual Abuse
of Boy Scouts a Valid Concern?"
Massachusetts News, 15 February 2001.
http://www.massnews.com/past_
issues/2001/march percent202001/
marboyrape.htm.

Farmer, Tom, and Laurel Sweet. "Reardon
Faces 122 Counts of Child Abuse
Indictment." *Boston Herald,* 1 August
2000, A1.

Felberbaum, Michael. "4 Boy Scout
Leaders Die at Jamboree." *Boston
Globe,* 26 July 2005. http://www.
boston.com/news/nation/articles/
2005/07/26/4_boy_scout_leaders_
die_at_jamboree.

Girl Scouts of America. "Safety and Risk
Management in Girl Scouting."

SafetyWise. New York: Girl Scouts of
America, 1993.

Gorran, Judy. *"Child Sexual Abuse,
Negligent Hiring and National
Fingerprint-Based Criminal History
Record Checks: The Evolving Duty Of
Reasonable Care."* National
Foundation to Prevent Child Sexual
Abuse to the Child Sexual Abuse
Litigation Group of the Association of
Trial Lawyers of America. http://www.
fbifingerprintchecks.com/hiring
.html.

Herman, K. C. "Appropriate Use of the
Child Abuse Potential Inventory in a
Big Brothers/Big Sisters Agency."
Journal of Social Service Research 20, 3/
4, 93–103. 1995.

Kapsourakis, Karen. "YMCA Settles Child
Abuse Suit." *The Daily Item,* 29 August
2002. http://www.thedailyitemoflynn
.com/news/all_news/sale_reardon
08292002.htm.

Kontorovich, E. V. "Scout's Honor."
National Review 50, no. 6 (6 April
1998): 40–42.

Lum, Matthew. "More Adults Needed to
Mentor Kids." *Foster's Daily Democrat,*
14 February 2002, C1.

Morlin, Bill. "West Tied to Sex Abuse in
'70s, Using Office to Lure Young Men."
Spokesman Review, 5 May 2005.
http://www.spokesmanreview.com/
jimwest/story.asp?ID=050505_
westmain.

Purdum, Todd. "California Justices Allow
Scouts to Bar Gay and Atheist

Members." *New York Times,* 24 March 1998, A1.

Ranalli, Ralph. "Families Sue Boy Scouts Over Sex Abuse." *Boston Globe,* 10 March 2000, B5.

Scouting For All. "Should I Let My Child Sign Up With the Boy Scouts of America?" http://www.scoutingfor all.org/aaic/shouldisign.shtml.

Scouts Alumni Association. "In the News." http://www.scoutsalumni. com.

Wood, Peregrin. "Boy Scouts Abuse Policy Crafted by Child Pornographer." *Irregular Times.* http://irregulartimes. com/index.php/archives/2005/03/ 30/boy-scouts-pornography-ring.

YMCA. "Child Abuse Prevention." http:// www.ymcamacon.org/Child percent 20Abuse percent20Prevention.htm.

Young, William. "Boy Scout Leader Arrested—Sexual Abuse." http:// www.davidicke.net/newsroom/ europe/england/062600a.html.

Chapter 7 Recreational Safety

Parents make big assumptions about how safe children are when they're at recreational facilities, as I learned the hard way. When I picked up my three-year-old from a morning summer recreation camp, the counselor invited my daughter to come back after lunch to watch a movie. I assumed the movie was a camp event and that the counselor would watch over her campers. The gym-turned-theater was bustling with kids of all ages. I sat my daughter and her friend with the rest of the kids from their unit. I asked the counselor when I should come back. When I returned at the time she gave me, I found the two girls waiting by themselves on the sidewalk. The film had gotten out early, and everyone had gone home. Only then did I learn that the film was not part of the camp program, but a special event in which the kids were on their own. Thankfully, an observant friend watched over them until I arrived, otherwise the results could have been disastrous.

Another time, I took my first- and third-grade children to play in the ocean with friends. Being from the Midwest, we knew nothing about ocean undertow. Naïvely, I put the kids on huge inflatable alligators to play on the waves. The no-lifeguard beach was filled with adults and children. Not one of them said a word to me about how flotation devices were a bad idea in the ocean. In a split second, the waves pulled them far from shore. In the seconds it took for me realize what was happening, they were washing further out to sea. People on the beach were engrossed in their own play and talk, and no one came to the rescue when I called for help. Picking up my new baby to avoid leaving her alone, I made the only choice I felt I had and ran into the high waves to pull them ashore. Poor judgment on my part and no assistance from others could have resulted in the drowning of my own children, as well as two of their friends. In both of these examples, other parents had trusted me to take good care of their children, and in both cases our pursuit of recreation could have been life-threatening.

Children need to play. It strengthens their cardiovascular and immune systems, releases brain endorphins, and increases social, mental, and physical health. But many recreational activities have an element of risk involved.

Parents assume that recreation programs have safeguards in place to prevent problems, and sometimes they do—but not always. What are the realistic risks of recreational activities?

On the surface, it appears that recreational programs must be safe, if for no other reason than that they would lose a lot of money if they were not. Recreation and amusement facilities are multimillion-dollar businesses that have become unofficial systems of child care. Thousands of children are dropped off by parents each day to spend hours at swimming pools, ski areas, golf courses, Chuck E. Cheese–type restaurants, zoos, amusement parks, museums, and nature areas. Unsupervised kids may spend summer days at the beach, afternoons at sporting events, or evenings at concerts. Adolescents may be dropped off at malls to shop alone for hours at a time. Employees at stores, parks, and recreation programs are all hired to do specific jobs that may not include the responsibility of watching over kids. Video arcade workers are paid to make sure the machines work and to exchange money for tokens, not to mind children. Librarians may be busy with other tasks and cannot oversee children every minute. Recreation businesses do try to create safe environments where kids don't get harassed, beaten-up, or robbed, but parents should not rely upon them to be babysitters. It is not necessarily safe for children to go to public places without adult supervision. It might feel safe because there are lifeguards or workers around, but parents ought not rely on a false sense of security. Even when there are adults present, children may get hurt, usually when adults overseeing them are inattentive, when the kids use poor judgment, or when equipment problems exist. It's time to turn to common types of recreation to assess their risk.

Amusement parks.

Over three hundred million people flock to more than six hundred amusement parks and attractions each year in the United States alone, including big ones like Disney, Six Flags, and Busch Gardens, smaller chains like Dollywood and Silver Dollar City, and local parks like Holiday World in Indiana, Cedar Point in Ohio, and Hershey Park in Pennsylvania. Some, like Story Land in New Hampshire, are designed with young children as the target audience, but most amusement facilities are designed for older children and adults. While some may have rides specifically for young children, most parks market their thrill rides to entice visitors and increase profits. Thrill rides may not be safe for younger children, which is why parks usually have age and height restrictions for them.

How many children get hurt at amusement parks and carnivals? We don't know, because there is no comprehensive source of such data. Historically, amusement parks and carnivals have not had federal safety standards, which gives individual park operators the ultimate responsibility for patrons' lives and limbs. When problems were reported to the Consumer Product Safety Commission, it started investigating and monitoring parks, which became safer as a result. But in 1981, as a result of lobbying by the amusement park industry and President Reagan's push for reduced federal control, amusement parks were removed from the Consumer Product Safety Commission's jurisdiction. As a result, park injuries and deaths have increased. In recent years the Commission has become more active, but there is still no federal law or national agency to require that ride operators file accident reports. Today, only eleven states have no rules for inspection of amusement park rides. Parks may report accidents to state authorities or insurance companies, but the reporting requirements aren't uniform, and the information may not be available to the public. Data on nonfatal injuries are difficult to obtain and often don't exist since minor injuries are seldom reported. State agencies report permanent amusement park ride injuries to the government, but there is no federal regulation of them. Congressman Frank Guarini of New Jersey pointed out that because there are no nationwide safety standards, American families play amusement ride roulette every time they go to a theme park. Uniform guidelines would help to ensure that all equipment is at the safest level for riders. States have varied dramatically in the safety standards held for carnivals and amusement parks, with some states imposing virtually no standards to assure safety for the millions of children and families who visit them.

Amusement parks are generally safer than small-town carnivals, which have rides that are installed and removed several times a week. Every time rides are set up, there is a new chance for mechanical and human errors that could put children at risk. Carnivals have a more transient employee pool, and workers may not be screened or supervised as carefully as those in amusement park settings. Statistical estimates released by the Consumer Product Safety Commission indicate the number of injuries suffered at traveling carnivals and fixed attractions like Disneyland in 2000 rose to 10,580 injuries sustained on roller coasters and other amusement-park rides, up from 7,185 emergency-room visits in 1993. The National Safety Council reported 15,914 yearly injuries from amusement park rides, but only 2 percent of injuries were serious enough to require hospitalization. On average, four nonoccupational fatalities on amusement rides occur each year nationwide. Federal reports for the year 2000 indicate a 33 percent increase of accidents from rides at a mobile carnival and a 57 percent increase for people injured at a fixed-site park. Children between the ages of ten and fourteen are the most susceptible to injury; teenagers are the next highest, while younger children are the least likely to be hurt. Females were hurt one-and-a-half more times than males. Fixed-site rides accounted for two-thirds of all injuries, but data is seldom collected on traveling amusement rides. Whirling rides and roller coasters were involved in the most deaths. The Wild Wonder roller coaster malfunctioned at Ocean City, N.J., killing a woman and her eight-year-old daughter after they were hurled from their car. Eight teens were killed when a fire engulfed a haunted house at a Six Flags Great Adventure park. At the Austin County Livestock Show and Rodeo, a fifteen-year-old girl died after a restraining bar on the Himalaya thrill ride broke, throwing her to the ground. Such lists go on and on.

People responsible for amusement park inspections may be elevator inspectors with no training in thrill rides, and they may not test rides for metal fatigue, which caused the crash of the Hell Hole ride in Coney Island and injured thirteen people. New amusement park rides designed to deliver bigger thrills have raised concerns that the higher speeds and stomach-wrenching drops could subject riders to greater risk. Cars on old-style roller coasters used to be lifted by chains or cables to the peak, where gravity would cause cars to accelerate downward. New coasters run on linear-induction motors, which allow the cars to be propelled by computer software–controlled magnetic energy. This is supposed to be an improvement, because park engineers can slow down the rides when necessary, but such technology also enables taller rides to go faster and turn upside down more times. Engineers design the swings, flips, and drops to create an illusion of risk. As rides have become bigger, faster, and scarier, doctors, regulators, and lawyers are saying that the danger is no longer imaginary. In recent years, claims of brain injury from roller coasters have increased. When one's head moves back and forth or up and down on rides, the brain can actually pull away from one side of the skull and slam into the other with enough force to break blood vessels. If blood pools in the space between the skull and brain, blood clots can create headaches, brain damage, or even death. Recent brain injuries associated with roller coasters have prompted the Brain Injury Association to launch an in-depth study of a possible connection, especially since children and teenagers accounted for six out of ten injuries. Policymakers and physicians recommend that the recreation industry or government regulate the speed and acceleration of giant coasters, as well as consider design improvements.

Water parks pose a special risk for children. Data do not indicate whether water parks are more dangerous than other types of amusement parks, but on average, two people die each year at them. From interviews with teenage employees of water parks, it appears that many near-drownings occur; many employees quit because they don't want to be responsible if something happens to a child. Water park attendance is around fifty-eight million visitors a year. Usually, human error is responsible for deaths and injuries when they occur, such as water slides that collapse because too many people try to go down them at the same time (often to break records). Sometimes problems occur due to mechanical error, staff training, or simple accidents, such as when ten people, including children, were injured or died at Six Flags Over Texas when the Roaring Rapids ride capsized, and occupants were unable to unbuckle their seat belts. The park did not require water rescue training for the staff at its water rides.

Among the rides at family fun centers, go-carts claim the highest frequency of accidents. Newer carts with side-by-side seats have been designed to avoid placing one rider in front of another. Sudden stops would frequently cause the rear passenger, typically the parent, to fall forward, pinning the front passenger, often a small child, against the steering wheel. Design improvements and rider restrictions have been encouraged by businesses such as the International Association of Amusement Parks and Attractions, Outdoor Amusement Business Association, International Association of Fairs and Exhibitions, National Association of Amusement Ride Safety Officials, and Amusement Manufacturers and Suppliers International. Some parks have hired consultants to improve the overall safety of their staff and facilities. Some parks have moved to using a coding system where patrons can identify the age of the rider, height, speed, expectancy, and movement. When organizations have safety structures in place, the risks are significantly reduced.

While accidents at amusement parks do occur, one has to assess relative risk. The National Safety Council found that approximately 300 million people visit fixed-site amusement parks each year. If each person goes on two rides, this means there are nearly 600 million rides occurring per year. The council estimates that the odds of being injured seriously enough to require hospital admission are about 1 in 7 million, and the odds of being fatally injured are 1 in 250 million. According to the Consumer Product Safety Commission, you're safer in an amusement park than using your home exercise equipment. The International Association of Amusement Parks and Attractions alleges that taking a ride on a coaster is safer than traveling by car to the grocery. On average 1.3 billion rides will be taken on roller coasters this year. The number of coaster deaths is quite small. While 12 people have died on amusement rides in California since 1973, 115,000 people died from traffic accidents there during the same period. Bret Lovejoy, president of the International Association of Amusement Parks and Attractions asserts that data prove there is virtually no safer form of recreation. Yet Kathy Dresslar of the Children's Advocacy Institute at the Center for Public Interest in Law in Sacramento stated that amusement parks often settle injury claims under the condition of secrecy, effectively hiding problems from the public. The A. M. Best Company reports that amusement parks, traveling carnivals, and water amusement rides have a general liability hazard index of 9, which is high. They allege the hazards are so high because individual states and even individual businesses have been allowed to set their own safety standards in lieu of the lack of federal regulation and enforcement of standards.

Yet less than 20 percent of all ride related injuries are caused by design, operation, or maintenance problems. Most injuries are caused by human error. Patron negligence, horseplay, and poor judgment are the cause of most accidents, not the condition or operation of the rides. Occasionally, bolts will become loose or unexpected problems with machinery may occur. Usually only deaths get reported; the near-misses don't. Known incidents are enough to make parents worry about safety of kids who attend amusement parks. The design of rides, their maintenance, and the competence of their operators are all related to human factors that can impact safety. Rides aren't the only risk for children; they can get lost, harassed, or abused if adults aren't around to supervise. Even the most attentive parents find that their children can wander off into a crowd in a blink of an eye. When this happened to my son, he knew to ask for help from a park employee, who took good care of him and delivered him back to me safely. But parents should realize that carnival and amusement park employees receive minimal training and work long hours in repetitive jobs that usually pay only minimum wage and no benefits. Inexperienced operators can be dangerous when they aren't attentive, which is common when staff turnover is high and employees are not trained to identify when kids are in trouble.

Swimming.

Parents often let their kids go with other kids to the beach or swimming pool assuming that they'll be safe under the watchful eyes of a lifeguard or another parent. But not all swimming facilities have lifeguards, and even if guards are present, accidents can still occur. Drowning and near-drowning are major causes of childhood mortality and injury in the United States. The National Safety Council reports that 4,500 drowning deaths occur each year, with young children and teens having the highest drowning rates. The U.S. Consumer Product Safety Commission conducted a study of drowning injuries and discovered three of every four submersion victims were between one and three years old, and two out of three were boys.

Beaches and swimming pools aren't the only places children drown. One-third of children drown in bathtubs, hot tubs, toilets, or buckets, especially top-heavy infants and toddlers who fall in headfirst. Even a dog's water bowl may be dangerous for an unsupervised child. Drowning is a quick and silent killer; in the time it takes to cross the room for a towel (ten seconds), a child in the bathtub can become submerged. In the time it takes to answer the phone (two minutes), that child can lose consciousness. In the time it takes to sign for a package at the door (four to six minutes), a child submerged in the pool can sustain permanent brain damage. For every child who drowns, there are eleven who nearly drown. These children may have long-term problems that range from fear of water to brain malfunctions due to oxygen deprivation while under water to spinal cord injuries that result in paralysis.

Parents let their children go to the beach with friends, relatives, and camp counselors, but this popular summer activity can also be one of the most perilous. According to interviews conducted with lifeguards at Atlantic Ocean beaches, people who are supposed to be watching kids frequently don't. Adults often situate their children in front of the lifeguard station assuming that the lifeguards will watch their children while they nap, swim, or talk with others. Babies seem especially at risk: their delicate skin puts them in danger of serious sunburn, they are unable to get out of the way of flying Frisbees, and running children may trip over them. One lifeguard I interviewed told me, "I guess parents just expect that we're here to monitor over everything. We can't. Our job is to constantly be scanning the waterfront in case someone is in danger of drowning." Another said "Lost kids come up to us all the time. They have no idea where their folks are, who obviously aren't watching them. I'll see people paying more attention to their dates or friends than the kids. And while there's a no alcohol policy on the beach, some folks drink and are in no condition to watch their kids in the water." Another lifeguard said, "what people do—and don't do—can be absolutely terrifying."

People who are unaware of the dangers of beaches and water can make foolish mistakes. Adults may think that swimmer's aides like water wings will keep kids afloat, but they are not substitutes for life jackets, and many experts disapprove of them since they give both adults and children a false sense of security. Even standing too close to the water can be dangerous for children, who can be picked up by a sneaker wave and washed into the sea. Sneaker waves appear without warning, often surging high up on the beach with deadly force and are impossible to predict. A rip is a strong current running out to sea between the shore and a sandbar and is the cause of most rescues performed at beaches. The larger the surf, the stronger the rip. Rips are dangerous for young, weak, or tired swimmers who can be easily swept into deep water.

Beaches aren't the only place where children are at risk of drowning; swimming pools can be very dangerous for children if they are not closely supervised. Nine-year-old Christina Transtamar drowned in her town swimming pool because the lifeguards didn't see her on the bottom of the diving area, and Krystal Brown drowned while swimming at a supervised YMCA facility. Most swimming pools have a rule that no child under the age of seven is allowed to swim unaccompanied by an adult, but with hundreds of children coming to the pool, it's almost impossible to enforce. According to one pool supervisor, "We keep our eye out as best we can for little kids who are here alone. Just recently there was this little girl who was being dropped off by her mother at 9:00 in the morning—four hours before we open. That happened for several days in a row. When we asked her how old she was, she said she was six." Other pool personnel have noticed that many children spend the day at the pool and have nothing to eat the entire day. Some lifeguards I interviewed talked about keeping a box of crackers available to give to such children, but they were uncomfortable feeding children, because they were afraid they could get in trouble. The line of what is appropriate care for employees to give to other people's kids is unclear.

Homes with private pools can also be dangerous when children are not closely supervised. Children may wander out of the house and fall into the pool, which is more likely when no fence surrounds it or if a gate to the pool area is left open. Toys floating in water are enticing to children who want to play with them. Some parents think their children are stronger swimmers than they actually are, and they may leave them unsupervised while they are inside doing chores. It only takes a moment for a child to drown. In most reported drownings, children were missing for less than five minutes when their bodies were discovered. Pool parties sometimes result in tragedy because adults are so busy talking to each other that no one sees children fall into the pool. Installation of four-sided fencing that isolates the pool from the house and the yard has been shown to decrease drownings of young children by 50 percent.

Playgrounds.

Playing at the park is a normal experience for kids. Most children love to go on slides, seesaws, swings, and monkey bars. Parents assume that kids will be safe when they go the local or school playground and that the equipment is safe and well maintained. Yet each year, over 267,000 children are injured on America's playgrounds, according to the National Safety Council. From January 1990 to August 2000, the Consumer Product Safety Commission received reports of 147 deaths of children younger than fifteen that involved playground equipment, and most injured children are under eight years old. On average, at least one child per month dies of playground equipment injuries and one child is injured every twenty-two minutes. The most common injuries are fractures, cuts, scrapes, strains, and sprains. Injuries to the head and face accounted for half of all injuries. When impact injuries to the neck and head occur, the potential for permanent neurological damage exists. Arm and hand injuries are common for older children. Falling was the most common cause of injuries.

Most playground injuries could have been avoided if adults monitored the children. In general, the risk of injury in playgrounds is low in comparison to the other risks to which children are exposed, and injury most often occurs when kids are reckless on the equipment or engaged in competitive peer situations with no adult referee. The higher the playground equipment, the more likely small children are to fall and get hurt. The National Program for Playground Safety advocates that parents actively supervise their children. Insurance companies recommend that playgrounds be regularly inspected to meet U.S. Consumer Product Safety Commission standards, such as slide height, cushioned areas underneath swings, well-secured equipment posts, and sturdy chains that will not pinch fingers.

Parents must assume ultimate responsibility for their children's safety in recreational situations. It is entirely possible for parents to select safe recreational activities for their children if they ask questions like the following:

Does the recreational facility seem well-run?

A quick scan gives parents lots of information about the probable safety of a recreational activity. Is it clean? Are employees available that seem competent? Do the facilities and equipment look well-maintained? Are signs visible to direct people where to go for help? These four criteria can be immediate indications of how attentive the facility is to important but less-visible safety features. If the facility passes the quick-scan test, parents can look for more detailed safety information.

Are there plenty of staff members around, and are they attentive?

If staff members are hard to find, if they seem preoccupied with other things, and if they don't seem competent, this is a bad sign. Most recreational facilities hire employees to do a particular job, such as selling ice cream or being a lifeguard, but they are still expected to look out for lost children or those who could get into trouble. Some beaches don't have lifeguards, which make them a poor choice for unsupervised swimmers. There may be wilderness guides available at nature parks, but they may have many miles of trails to cover, so it is unrealistic to assume that they can be available in short order for people who need help. People who work at recreational facilities should be trained to know a good deal about them, which means park supervisors should know the trails well, and amusement park attendants should know the rides. They should also have good "people sense" and be attentive to behaviors that could lead children toward danger.

Never let your child swim alone or without a good adult swimmer available.

The U.S. Lifesaving Association's motto is "always swim near a lifeguard." If there is no lifeguard available at beaches, pools, or water-parks, then children and youth should be accompanied by a strong adult swimmer who knows how to help in case of an emergency. The National Safety Council recommends that supervising adults constantly scan children and be able to reach them within twenty seconds. Drownings usually happen quickly, and there is rarely splashing or noise to alert anyone. If the adults are not strong swimmers or the water is deeper than they are tall, well-intended caregivers are not qualified to watch children playing in the water. Supervisors should know how to perform CPR and should never drink alcohol while children are swimming, because it may impair their ability to help kids in an emergency.

Assess amusement ride safety.

Before allowing a child to go on a particular ride, it's a good idea to watch the ride in action. Look for creaky joints, moving pieces, and the competence of the operator. Avoid rides that appear worn or not put together securely. There should be instructions and health warnings posted for each ride; some rides have age and size restrictions, and if children are too short, tall, large, or thin to fasten all safety harnesses properly, don't let them take the ride. See if the ride operators hook riders in securely and if they watch the reactions of the riders, in case riders get sick or scared. Be particularly careful at carnivals, since employees may be more transient, and equipment is set up and taken down dozens of times each year.

Check the environment.

Is the weather appropriate for the activities to be undertaken? If not, don't do it. Hikes in bad weather, canoe rides on choppy water, or leaving kids to ski in frigid conditions could put them in harm's way. Look at the physical environment of the recreation area. If its grounds are run-down, it may be a sign that the management isn't paying proper attention to its operation. Recreational facilities may also have social environments with certain groups of people attending them frequently. If parents observe individuals at the recreation site who make them feel uncomfortable, then children should not be left there unsupervised.

Behavior considerations.

Sometimes children and adults act irresponsibly. Excitement, peer pressure, and the desire to prove oneself are all factors that make younger, inexperienced, or less-mature children subject to higher risk. Most accidents at recreational facilities are due to poor judgment or human error, so parents and children should be encouraged to use good prevention strategies. Some are simple: young children sometimes shouldn't do certain things, like hiking hard or long trails, swimming in deep water, or standing up on seated amusement rides. If they have health problems, especially heart or back problems, some activities should be avoided. Misbehavior and horseplay get kids into trouble. Kids who don't use moderation and continue to play even when they feel dizzy, motion sick, or energy depleted are more likely to get into trouble.

Designated parent.

When kids go on recreational outings, whether at the beach or the amusement park, a parent should go along to make sure that they are safe. Don't let children go to recreational facilities by themselves. This is never a good idea, especially when children are young and prone to immature judgment, but older children can get into trouble too, especially with peers or people who they meet at the recreational facility. A designated adult can identify risky situations, monitor interactions, and get help in an emergency. Designated parents know the kids and provide needed insulation between them and employees and patrons.

Teach kids what to do if they get lost.

It is impossible to watch children every second, especially when parents try to give them chances to learn independence. Children can get confused about which way to turn to find their parents after they get off an amusement ride; they may take the wrong spur on a hiking trail and end up lost in the woods; or they may be unable to find their family among the sea of people sunbathing at the beach. Children should know their name, phone number, address, and how to find help when they don't see anyone they know.

PROMISING PROGRAMS

Despite the lack of federal standards and oversight, the recreation industry has actively pursued the creation of safer activities and facilities. When clear polices and standards are implemented and monitored, potential problems can be avoided. Fear of litigation has been a positive force to motivate recreational facilities to become safer. Many amusement parks have changed their policies on unsupervised children and require that there be a responsible adult available to authorize treatment, in case kids get hurt. If recreational facilities do not have the appropriate mechanisms available to ensure reasonable safety for patrons of all ages, parents have a responsibility of either encouraging them to create them or avoiding such activities. While suing recreation businesses may result in the implementation of better safeguards, the fact is that parents must take responsibility for making sure their children are competent enough to manage the recreational event. If children cannot swim, parents have no business letting them go to water events. If children wish to hike, they should stay together and not wander off alone. If they ride amusements, they should do so responsibly. Children are the responsibility of parents, not recreational organizations. Each must do its part.

RESOURCES

A.M. Best Worldwide Global Headquarters
Ambest Road
Oldwick, NJ 08858
(908) 439-2200
http://www.ambest.com

Amusement Manufacturers and
Suppliers International
1250 S.E. Port St. Lucie Blvd., Suite C
Port St. Lucie, FL 34952
(772) 398-6701
http://www.aimsintl.org

Center for Public Interest Law in
Sacramento
717 K Street, Suite 509
Sacramento, CA 95814
(916) 444-3875
http://www.cpil.org

El Cajon Firefighter's Association
Drowning Fact Sheet
100 E. Lexington Ave.
El Cajon, CA 92029
(619) 441-1615
http://www.elcajonfirefighters.org/
drownings.htm

Foundation for Aquatic Injury
Prevention
11230 White Lake Rd.
Fenton, MI 48430
(800) 342-0330
http://aquaticisf.org/pool-safety.htm

International Association of Amusement
Parks and Attractions
1448 Duke Street
Alexandria, VA 22314
(703) 836-4800
http://www.iaapa.org

International Association of Fairs and
Exhibitions
PO Box 985
Springfield, MO 65801
(417) 862-5771
http://www.fairsandexpos.com

National Association of Amusement
Ride Safety Officials
PO Box 638
Brandon, FL 33509-0638
(813) 661-2779
http://www.naarso.com

National Parent Teacher Association
541 N. Fairbanks Court
Suite 1300
Chicago, IL 60611-3396
(312) 670-6782
(800) 307-4782
http://www.pta.org

National Program for Playground Safety
School of HPELS, WRC 205
University of Northern Iowa
Cedar Falls, IA 50614-0618
(800) 554-PLAY
http://www.uni.edu/playground

National Safe Kids Campaign
1301 Pennsylvania Ave., NW, Suite 1000
Washington, DC 20004
(202) 662-600
http://www.safekids.org/tier2_rl.
cfm?folder_id=181

National Safety Council
1121 Spring Lake Drive
Itasca, IL 60143-3201
(630) 285-1121
http://www.nsc.org

Outdoor Amusement Business
Association
1035 S. Semoran Blvd., Suite 1045A
Winter Park, FL 32792
(800) 517-OABA or (407) 681-9444
http://www.oaba.org

Red Cross Health and Safety Tips
2025 E Street, NW
Washington, DC 20006
(202) 303-4498
http://www.redcross.org/services/hss/
tips/healthtips/safetywater.html

State of Oregon
Beach Safety Tips
Oregon Parks and Recreation
Department
725 Summer Street, NE, Suite C
Salem, OR 97301
(503) 986-0707
http://www.oregonstateparks.org/
beach_tips.php

Statistics on Pediatric Drownings
University of South Florida
4202 E. Fowler Ave.
Tampa, FL 33620
(813) 974-2001
http://hsc.usf.edu/CLASS/JulieJ/
Statistics.htm

U.S. Consumer Product Safety
Commission
4330 East-West Highway
Bethesda, MD 20814
(301) 504-7923
http://www.cpsc.gov

U.S. Lifesaving Association
(866) 367-8752
http://www.usla.org

REFERENCES

Alliston, Sue. "The Nuts and Bolts of
    Amusement Park Safety for This
Summer's High Riders." *Life* 8 (August
    1985): 32.

American Academy of Pediatrics. "Drowning in Infants, Children and Adolescents." *Pediatrics* 92, no. 2, (August 1993): 292–294. http://www.aap.org/policy/04482.html.

Arnold, David, and Diana Raschke. "Five Hurt in Roller-Coaster Collision at NH Park." *Boston Globe,* 28 July 2001, B1.

Ball, David. *"Playground Risks."* http://www.hse.gov.uk/research/crr_htm/2002/crr02426.htm.

Barratt, Martin. "Ride at Your Own Risk." *Professional Safety* 43, no. 3 (March 1998): 32–38.

"Brain Injuries." http://www.staysafe.info/newsletter_05_2002.html.

Chew, Cassie. "Computers Create New Excitement, Safety in Amusement Park Attractions." *Fort Worth Star Telegram,* 22 March 1999, A4.

Consumer Product Safety Commission." *Pools Are Not the Only Drowning Danger at Home for Kids: Data Show Other Hazards Cause More than 100 Residential Child Drowning Deaths Annually."* 23 May 2002. Press release no. 02–169. http://www.cpsc.gov/cpscpub/prerel/prhtml02/02169.html.

Cooper, Hollie. *"Amusement Parks—An American Pastime."* 19 June 2000. http://www.superpages.com/articles/article-06–30–00_2.html.

Furtell, Jim. " Rider Responsibility Legislation Picking Up Speed." *Amusement Business* 109, no. 18 (5 May 1997):26–29.

Gips, Michael. "Amusement Bemusement." *Security Management* 41, no. 10 (October 1997): 12–14.

Hanley, Robert. "NJ Roller Coaster that Killed Mother and Child Had Problems Earlier, Riders Report." *New York Times,* 31 August 1999, A20.

Hirsch, Jerry. "California Theme Park Bill Could Meet Resistance." *Orange County Register,* 24 February 1999, A1.

———. "Second California Theme Park Bill Would Let Operators Inspect Own Rides." *Orange County Register,* 25 February 1999, A4.

Kertesz, Louise. "Public Water Parks Not the Safety Threat They Once Were." *Business Insurance,* 26, no. 22 (1 June 1992): 3–5.

Klein, Rick. "One Killed, 10 Injured as Amusement Boat Ride Capsizes." *Dallas Morning News,* 2003. http://gw3.epnet.com/fulltext/asap?results.=&filter=&deth=437&Forward.x=2&Forward.

Muret, Don. "Old Indiana Accident Still Looms with Tough New Safety Laws." *Amusement Business* 100, no. 2 (12 January 1998): 28–30.

O'Brien, Tim. "Industry Reacts to E. Coli Incident at Georgia Waterpark." *Amusement Business* 110, no. 26 (29 June 1998): 26.

———. "More Park Employees Attend AIMS Seminar." *Amusement Business* 110, no. 4 (26 June 1998): 20.

———. "The Statistics: How Safe Are Parks?" *Amusement Business* 109, no. 21 (26 May 1997): 27.

O'Connor, Dennis, and Jennifer Swenson. "Safety and Oversight of Amusement Rides in California." August 1997. http://www.library.ca.gov/CRB/97/12/.

Pearce, Fred. "Not All Fun at the Fair: Inadequate Safety at British Fairgrounds." *New Scientist* 135,no. 1836 (29 August 1992): 25–30.

Perlman, Ellen. "Carnival Jitters." *Governing* 11, no, 10 (16 July 1998): 7.

Petite-Zerman, Sophie. "Are Children Not Having Enough Fun?" *Utne Reader.* September–October 2002. http://www.utne.com. 2002.

Polaneczky, Ronnie. "Killer Rides: The Scary Truth About Amusement Parks." *Redbook* 187, no. 4 (August 1996): 102–105.

Ray, Susan. "Attractions Becoming Babysitters: Minors Presenting Major Dilemmas." *Amusement Business* 105, no. 32 (9 August 1993): 3–5.

"Report on Playground Safety in the UK." *Exchange Every Day.* 452 (27 August 2002). http://www.ChildCareExchange .com. 2002.

"Safety, Liability Issues Fuel Changes in the Go-Kart Industry." *Amusement Business* 106, no. 3 (17 January 1994): 23.

Schweizer, Peter, and Rochelle Schweizer. *Disney: The Mouse Betrayed.* Regency Park, Australia: Regnery Publishing Co., 2002.

Sullivan, Andy. "Amusement Park Injuries Continue to Climb." *Reuters.* 23 August 2000. http://www.thestandard.com/ wire/0,2231,28113,00.html.

Tinsworth, Deborah, and McDonald, Joyce. *Special Study: Injuries and Deaths Associated with Children's Playground Equipment.* Washington, D.C.: U.S. Consumer Product Safety Commission, April. 2001.

Tirado, Leo. "Amusement Park Patrons Must Keep Safety in Mind." *Business Journal Serving San Jose and Silicon Valley* 15, no. 51 (13 April 1998): 31.

Van Natta, Don. "Thrill Ride Inspections in New York Are Faulted." *New York Times,* 6 August 1995, A1.

Waddell, Ray. "Guests, Park Share Responsibility for Safety." *Amusement Business* 109, no. 40 (6 October 1997: 25.

Wojcik, Joanne. "Disney World Doesn't Goof Around With Safety." *Business Insurance* 32, no. 18 (4 May 1998): 39.

Wood, Sean. "Procedures and Safety at Six Flags to be Reviewed." *Fort Worth Star Telgram,* 14 April 1999, 13.

Yoshino, Kimi . "A New Fear for Roller Coaster Riders." *Boston Globe,* 9 June 2002, A18.

Chapter 8 How Safe Are Kids at Camp?

High school student Thomas Nazarro looked forward to ice-climbing, kayaking, and mountain hiking in an Alaska summer wilderness program. He was so adept that he was given the designation of an advanced camper and was allowed the opportunity to adventure, unsupervised, for a week with other campers. One afternoon, Thomas went to fetch water from a nearby stream. When he did not return, the other campers retraced his steps. They found his bucket beside the frozen stream. They surmised that he slipped into an icy moulin and tumbled down an endless tunnel beneath the water's surface. It took time for camp officials to be contacted, time for help to arrive at the scene, and time to lower a camera on a long cable down the hole to look for his body, which was never found. Although the camp program was investigated and was not found negligent, his friends and family grieve over his needless loss. Thomas was more than a statistic. This loving and joyful boy was one of my son's best friends. He ate and slept overnight at my house, played in my woods, and had pizza birthday parties with us. A volunteer fire-man, he was adored by everyone. He and his family had counted on the adults in charge of the camp to create a safe experience so he would not get hurt. Instead, Thomas is dead, and his family and friends are heartbroken.

Camp can be a wonderful opportunity for children to discover their potential and investigate the world around them. Experts at the American Psychological Association and American Academy of Pediatrics regard summer camp as a building block to the successful development of children and youth. A good camp experience can increase a child's self-esteem and confidence, which can decrease problems like substance abuse, interpersonal violence, and inappropriate behavior. Camp helps children to become independent, make friends, build character, and overcome obstacles. Trained counselors may be able to help campers resolve serious personal issues. Some kids come to camp concerned about home or health problems and some have found it difficult to be accepted at school and view camp as a fresh start to make new friends. Camps can offer opportunities for fun, health, relaxation and the development of athletic, artistic, academic. and interpersonal skills. Camps usually have one counselor to every seven campers, while the ratio at schools is typically one teacher to twenty-five students. Counselors are with campers through the entire day and get to know them well and are in a good position to help them. These benefits can best be achieved when parents select the right camp for their children. Camps are not equal in program, quality, or safety.

Camps are expected to be challenging but not unsafe. While most children laughingly remember camp songs and adventures, some recall horrible, life-altering experiences. For instance, at church Camp Fatima in New Hampshire, Father Ronald Paquin molested altar boys; at a Massachusetts summer football camp, older players hazed younger ones; athlete Adam Dzialo cannot speak or walk following a near-drowning accident in the Deerfield River at the Adventure Unlimited camp, which was unlicensed and understaffed.

Are these experiences common or unusual? Each summer over six million children go to camp. Camping provides much more than summer sleep-away experiences, and many camps focus on special skill development in sports, music, or academics. The camping industry has become a big business, with parents spending over eleven billion dollars annually. According to the National Camping Association, there are ten thousand day or resident camps throughout the United States. Most are privately owned and operated family businesses; about a quarter are run by nonprofit organizations, such as the YMCA or Scouts. Other camps are run by agencies, religious and fraternal organizations, municipal government, educational institutions, or corporations such as Nike.

Over a half-million people are employed in the camp industry as counselors, program or activity leaders, administrators, maintenance, food service, and health care providers. While some employees have a background in camping, administration, education, or child care, most are young workers who don't make much money but view camp work as summer fun. Most camp counselors earn about one thousand dollars per summer, or an average of eighty-three dollars a week, working more than forty hours per week for a twelve-week season. Risk is a realistic concern anytime employees are inexperienced, underpaid, not heavily monitored, and put in long hours working with youth.

Camp work is unlike other forms of youth work because most interactions with campers takes place in cabins, one-on-one talks, or in other settings where typically no administrator is present. What parents or administrators observe may not be representative of what really goes on behind the scenes at camp. Glitzy brochures advertise the benefits of the camp; they are not designed to alert parents of potential problems. While size of the camp, well-equipped buildings, lovely landscaping, and new canoes may be attractive, the most important factor in camp quality is the staff. According to the American Camping Association (ACA), camp advertisements promote glowing descriptions and breathtaking photos with exciting activities to entice campers. In the end, it is the staff attentiveness and interaction that determines the quality of the camp program. Sensitive, competent staff members are more important than the surroundings. Counselor skill is especially important in camps like Seeds of Peace, which bring together children from different cultures to gain a greater understanding of one another. While it's good for children to experience new ways of thinking and doing things, mixing people with different attitudes may be problematic unless deftly handled. In short, there are a variety of factors that are responsible for make-or-break experiences for campers.

TYPES OF CAMPS

The camp industry's original focus was to provide outdoor summer recreation. According to the National Camping Association, camp is no longer confined to the traditional concept of swimming lessons, campfire sing-alongs, and disparaging comments about the food. Experiences span sports, adventure, travel, culture, and intellectual development. Camps can teach kids how to build a computer, learn foreign languages, perfect musical ability, sail, learn theater and fine arts, skate, dog sled, learn horsemanship, or lose weight. Kids can become junior archeologists, environmentalists, astronauts, golfers, or tennis pros. Because of the range of camps, parents must assess their child's skills and personality. Sports camps are not suitable for nonathletic children; adventure camps may not be appropriate for shy, introverted children. Kids can be set up for failure or success in their camp experiences. While each program is unique, camps can be broken down into the following types:

Day camps.

Day camps open in the morning and end around dinnertime, corresponding to most parents' work schedules. Most day camps have a particular program focus, are co-ed, and are geared toward specific age groups. They are run by schools, community recreation departments, civic groups, and nonprofit organizations and use high school or college students as counselors. Many are not ACA accredited.

Resident camps.

At resident camps, also known as sleepaway camps, children stay for extended periods of time and participate in a variety of activities. Camps can be co-ed or single-gendered, and while most set eight as the minimum age, some accept children as young as four. Residential camp programs can include general camp experiences or focus on specialty areas like sports, academics, health, wilderness exposure, or therapy.

General camps.

General camps are cafeteria-style camps, which provide children with a little taste of everything. Usually campers swim, canoe, hike, do arts and crafts, engage in drama and music activities, and try their hand at archery. General camps are good introductions for children who have never been to camp before. Organizations like the YMCA and 4-H are famous for their general camp programs. However, campers increasingly select specialty camps.

Arts camps.

Camps with an artistic focus promote the development of music, drama, dance, painting, ceramics, photography, and other aesthetic skills. For instance, Interlochen's music camps are famous for catering to young musicians who are interested in orchestra performance. Many communities have summer theater programs in which children learn performance art and create an open-to-the-public play to highlight their skills at the end of camp.

Sports camps.

Sports camps are designed to help young athletes become proficient in soccer, basketball, volleyball, soccer, football, hockey, swimming, and equestrian sports, as well as in aquatics, archery, fencing, skating, golf, gymnastics, baseball, biking, swimming, and tennis. Sports camps vary dramatically in structure and focus. They may be sponsored by schools or universities, private organizations (the Boulder Brook Stables), corporations (like Adidas), or professional teams (like Major League Ball teams). Staff training standards may differ from one camp to another, but sports camps have the acquisition of skills, team behavior, and how to be competitive as their primary focus. While sports camps can be fun and teach children a great deal about how to be successful athletes, they can also put a significant amount of stress on them, both physically and emotionally. Children need competent and caring counselors to help them work through these issues successfully. If children get injured or discouraged, they may lose interest in the very sport for which they went to camp. It's imperative that kids who go to sports camps get a clean bill of health from their doctors before they go, otherwise undiagnosed health conditions could erupt into serious problems.

Academic camps.

There are so many interesting things to learn that it is impossible for schools to teach them all. If kids want to learn more about a particular topic or need specialized training, academic camps may be good options for them. Academic camps range widely. Children can learn marine biology on a seafaring vessel, orate Shakespeare on the stage at his Strafford-upon-Avon theater, or produce their own film. Other academic camps teach intricate technological or computer skills or the ins and outs of the stock market. Some, like the Wolfeboro Camp School in New Hampshire, emphasize positive reinforcement to student-campers, who leave with improved self-discipline, better study skills, and greater self-confidence in their ability to succeed.

Health camps.

Children who have had serious health conditions may find themselves safer and more comfortable in camps that are designed to address their particular health needs. Today there are camps for children with respiratory ailments, attention deficit disorders, AIDS, autism, blood disorders, cancer, cerebral palsy, cystic fibrosis, diabetes, epilepsy, hearing impairments, behavior problems, emotional problems, mental retardation, mobility limitations, multiple sclerosis, muscular dystrophy, speech impairments, spina bifida, substance abuse, and visual impairments. Health camps may also focus on weight loss or helping youth with eating disorders. The staff members at these types of camps are usually well-trained with how to deal with those medical issues and the camp's facilities are structured to accommodate the specific needs of the campers. There is a big difference between traditional camps that are willing to accept "special needs campers" and camps that specialize in particular health problems.

Religious camps.

Many religious organizations run camps to provide children faith-in-action opportunities, where campers are exposed to traditional camp experiences with a theological twist. The camps mirror the faith's beliefs, so it is important that the children want to participate in activities that reflect the faith's philosophy and practices.

Wilderness camps.

Wilderness camps are also known as outdoor adventure programs. Campers may hike the Appalachian Trail, canoe down the Saco River in Maine, or ride horseback through the mountains of the Southwest. The outdoor adventure camps are designed to challenge children while providing them with aesthetic experiences in natural environments. Most are in remote locations, so parents must be aware of prevention plans and how the staff is trained to handle emergencies.

International experience camps.

A variety of summer camps provide children with the opportunity to travel to other countries. While they are usually very expensive, these camps expose children to different cultures through sightseeing, academic, leisure, and sporting activities.

Community service camps.

Camps that encourage youth to do something for the benefit of someone else have popped up around the country and are a hot new camp market, comprising about 20 percent of the American Camping Association's 2,400 accredited camps. These camps give youth the chance to volunteer their services to gain academic credit and job or college references or to broaden their perspectives. Some "campers" do food drives or yard work in their local communities, others travel to build housing in deprived areas of the United States. Campers at Florida's Lifeworks International camp spend three weeks working with orphans in China, or they may teach children at a Costa Rican school. While youth volunteer their services, their parents pay upwards of $3,600 for them to have this opportunity. The Global Works camp in Pennsylvania takes teens to Fiji to build huts for ecotourism, while campers with Putney Student Travel may pay $7,000 a month to help farmers in Tanzania. While there are benefits for children to experience altruism, the financial costs to parents are significant, as are the safety factors of sending children around the world under the care of people the parents have never met.

Therapy camps.

The use of camps to provide therapy for troubled children and rebellious youth has increased significantly in recent years. Many have a wilderness focus and are located in the western part of the United States. Children may be placed in challenging conditions in order to break bad habits. Therapy camps advertise that they can instill confidence, self-esteem, and humility in troubled youth. Hundreds of therapy camps exist nationwide, but many are controversial because they implement strategies that defy conventional norms of camp safety. For instance, some therapy camps have been accused of abusing campers, denying them food, and placing them in the control of counselors whose intervention strategies may be unorthodox or even dangerous. For instance, sixteen-year-old Paul Choy became comatose after Rite of Passage camp staff used excessive force and restraints, and Pathfinders, a New Mexico program for troubled teens, was forced to shut down after campers were beaten, cursed at, made to sleep without blankets, hiked twelve miles a day, and forced to carry fecal matter or eat their own vomit as punishment for misbehavior.

HOW TO CHOOSE A CAMP

It's important to select the right camp situation for a child, since camps and children vary considerably. There are clear-cut, simple steps that parents can take to increase the likelihood that their children will have a wonderful camp adventure. These include:

Identify what your child—and you—need from a camp experience.

What you need determines what kind of camp to look for. Do parents want their children to go to camp for a vacation, an educational experience, or to keep the kids busy while the parents work? Do you want a general, all-purpose camp or a specialty camp? What types of experiences do the children want to gain, and what types do parents want to avoid? Is day or residential camp preferable? How long is the camp needed: a week, a month, or all summer? First-time campers do better with a shorter camping experience, while seasoned campers may prefer a longer, more-challenging camping experience. Can the child handle a sleep-away experience? Does the child have special physical, emotional, social, cognitive, or health needs that influence what is needed? Some camps are highly structured, while others allow campers to select their own activities.

Do your research.

Parents can find useful information about camps from web-based searches or local community information and referral offices. Organizations like 4-H, the Scouts, and the YMCA have multiple camp programs and locations from which to choose. The American Camping Association provides detailed descriptions of hundreds of accredited camps. The ACA requires that camps meet standards such as having emergency transportation available at all times, first aid facilities, aquatic programs supervised by certified staff, health histories for all campers and staff, emergency exits from second-floor sleeping quarters, and multiple exits from any dwelling. Some camps, including many wonderful ones, feel they don't need ACA accreditation, but they can still provide parents with some reassurance, especially if the camp is unlicensed and uninspected. Most camps will send brochures, videotapes, and other materials, but remember, this information is designed to attract prospective campers. If they don't mention being accredited, it's probably because they aren't. Parents can also contact state-run organizations such as the police department or public health department to determine if the camps are clean and safe.

Check out the camp!

Every camp has its own focus and philosophy. At a minimum, parents should talk to the director of the camp to determine whether it is the right place for their children. Whenever possible, the family should go visit the prospective camp to see for themselves how it is run and whether it fits their needs. Watch the counselors in action, talk with campers, observe facilities, and look at the schedule of activities. Are the cabins designed to give your child privacy to shower, toilet, and dress? Do the sleeping accommodations prevent sexual abuse? Does the camp's philosophy complement your own parenting philosophy? What kinds of activities do they promote, and do they fit your children's personality and needs? While some camps have an ongoing philosophy that guides them generation after generation, others change each season under the direction of new administrators. Camps today may include children who come from other countries, cultures, races, or religious groups.

Some children may find themselves uncomfortable with people who are different, so this increases the need for staff sensitivity.

Analyze the cost.

The costs for camps vary widely, from $15 a day for programs run by community or nonprofit groups to over $1,500 a week for private camps. Good, inexpensive camps can be found, but parents should look carefully at the costs and benefits before they select a camp. Beyond the financial costs there are personal costs; sometimes camps inadvertently put kids at risk because they do not have big enough operating budgets to purchase quality resources or to give their counselors time off. Camp costs may also include sleeping bags, hiking equipment, canteen money, and clothing, so parents should remember to add those into cost of the overall camp experience.

How competent is the staff?

Staff competence is the single most important consideration when leaving children for an extended period of time. What are the qualifications of the directors and counselors? How long have they worked there? If staff have worked at the same camp for many years, this speaks of a success record; if there is a staff turnover rate of more than 50 percent, something could be amiss. There should be a mix of older and younger counselors, since younger staff may not know how to deal with children or crises. Ask for a copy of the staff's training curriculum to see if it addresses topics like homesickness, bed-wetting, and how to handle interpersonal problems. It is useful for parents to anticipate how camp staff will protect campers from injury and abuse. Common camp situations that require a deft hand on the part of staff include girls starting their period, vomiting, and homesickness. Bed-wetting is embarrassing for children and must be handled discretely.

Mature staff judgments can prevent problems, while poor decisions can put children at risk. Camper safety relies upon counselor competence: don't take kids out in bad weather, make sure they are properly dressed and that they don't get lost when on the trails, lock away food so bears don't invade, and require safety belts and billets when rock climbing.

What is the ratio of staff-to-campers?

Younger campers need more contact with staff, so their ratios should be lower than older campers, who are more self-sufficient. There should be one staff member for every six campers for children younger than twelve; the ratios for older children can increase to one counselor for every eight campers. Day camps have higher ratios than residential camps. Two staff members should be required for most activities in order to prevent problems.

What percentage of campers return?

Good camps find themselves swamped with waiting lists and campers who return year after year. If a camp has a high camper turnover rate, there may be a reason why kids don't want to return.

How are health issues addressed?

Children may return home from camp tanned, more muscular, and with greater aerobic capacity, but most campers get their share of bites, scrapes, burns, allergies, sunburns, splinters, food reactions, communicable disorders—like gastroenteritis or respiratory tract infections—and excessive cold or heat exposure. Usually these problems can be prevented or handled successfully if camp staff is prepared. Broken bones, sprains, torn ligaments, concussions, cuts, bruises, and exertion problems are less common but can happen. Many campers have health problems; studies have found that almost half of campers are on regular medication. Legally, camps must make sure medications are dispensed and used properly. During a hike, asthmatic Jovahny Ortiz, age fourteen, died after he had an attack and couldn't access his inhaler, which was locked up safely in the nurse's office back at camp.

The American Academy of Pediatrics recommends that each camper and staff member have a health record on file. They also encourage camps to have quick access to a licensed physician or nurse and a daily health surveillance protocol to ensure cleanliness in washrooms, laundry, toilets, sleeping areas, food storage, and food preparation areas. Basic cleanliness should not be assumed, as I learned when I stopped in the bathroom where my daughter was attending a privately run camp and found razor blades, scissors, and open containers of medicine on the counter of the sink. Since one never knows when accidents will happen, camps should have readily available written procedures for handling health emergencies, accidents, and disasters, as well as search and rescue procedures for missing persons. Parents may also want to know about the quality and quantity of the food, polices about meat, the presence of nuts, or vegetarian alternatives.

What are the camp's water safety policies?

Water is a concern for parents and camps alike. Many campers are not good swimmers but want to swim or go out in boats. Balancing water fun and safety can be challenging, and camp staff must be extraordinarily careful to supervise campers and avoid putting them in risky situations. Some camps specialize in water activities, such as learning how to surf the ocean, kayak, whitewater raft, or learn underwater archeology. These water-specific activities require significant attention. Other camps are beside lakes or rivers where campers can fish, wade, or paddle at their leisure with little or no staff supervision. Parents are encouraged to learn about how camps handle water activities, but they must also assess their children's swimming skills and emotional ability to make mature decisions when they are around water.

How does the camp handle discipline?

It is natural for children to make mistakes, so it is incumbent upon staff to discipline them in instructive, but not punitive, ways. It is important to find out the camp's policies for dealing with problematic behavior. While most camps use a warning-before-dismissal policy, some camps, especially those designed for "behavior modification," may use physical force as an institutionalized part of their program procedures.

PROMISING PROGRAMS

The Circus Smirkus Vermont camp is a model of high-quality care for kids. It pays close attention to its programs, staff, diet, facilities, and management of day-to-day activities. Circus Smirkus gives kids a chance to run away and join the circus with their parents' blessings. Since 1987, they have provided a format for youths and adults to collaborate in life-enhancing adventures through the circus arts. The camp strives to help children and teens to achieve personal excellence. Being a circus performer requires self-control and personal strength, and children who attend camp leave it stronger physically, emotionally, and socially. Smirkus teaches children that hard work, self-discipline, and demanding performance can benefit them at camp and in their everyday lives. It is run by a director and set of counselors who have been campers there themselves, and technical instruction is provided by professional circus coaches and performers who come from multicultural backgrounds. Children from all over the world are given the opportunity to

immerse themselves in artistic productions by putting together circus perfor-
mances. Dreams come true at this delightful summer camp, but this outcome
requires intense administration and management, supervision, anticipation
of potential problems, and the establishment of positive prevention practices.

RESOURCES

American Academy of Pediatrics
141 Northwest Point Blvd.
Elk Grove Village, IL 60007
(847) 434-4000
http://www.aap.org

American Camping Association
5000 State Road 67 North
Martinsville, IN 46151
(800) 428-CAMP
http://www.aca-camps.org

Camp Safety
http://www.campsafetyguide.com

Christian Camping International
http://www.cciworldwide.org/home/
htm

Hobart and William Smith Colleges
Summer Programs
311 Pulteney Street
Geneva, NY 14456
http://www.hws.edu/about/summer
progs/faqs.asp

MedicineNet.com
Keeping Kids Safe at Summer Camp
http://www.medicinenet.com/script/
main/art.asp?articlekey=51675

National Association of Therapeutic
Wilderness Camps
698 Dinner Bell-Ohiopyle Road
Ohiopyle, PA 15470
http://www.natwc.org

National Camping Association
610 Fifth Ave.
PO Box 5371
New York, NY 10185
http://www.summercamp.org/
index2.html

Peterson's Education Center
2000 Lennox Dr.
PO Box 67005
Lawrenceville, NJ 08648
http://www.petersons.com

REFERENCES

American Academy of Pediatrics.
   "Medical Guidelines for Day Camps
   and Residential Camps." *Pediatrics* 87,
   no. 1 (1991): 117–119.

Associated Press. "Agencies Probe Camp
   for Disabled." *Boston Globe*, 1 August
   1999, A36.
Baker, Al. "Family Mourns at Edge of River

Where Boys Are Presumed Lost." *New York Times*, 15 August 2000, A22.

Ball, Armandand Beverly. *Basic Camp Management: An Introduction to Camp Administration*. Martinsville, Ind.: American Camping Association, 1995.

Benn, Reuel, and Jacob Goldberg. *The Camp Counselor*. New York: McGraw Hill, 1951, 41.

Brody, Jane. "Summer Camp Scrutiny a Must for Parents." *Fosters Sunday Citizen*, 6 June 1999, 3E.

Carbone, Ray. "Camp Drug Regs Eyed in Wake of Death." *Fosters Daily Democrat*, 7 July 2002, 5A.

Fichman, Laura, Richard Koestner, and David Zuroff. "Dependency and Distress at Summer Camp." *Journal of Youth and Adolescence* 26, no. 2 (1997): 217–232.

Godbey, Suan Flagg. "Head Off Homesickness." *Prevention Magazine* (August 1996) : 44.

Hammond, Pat. "Staff's Role in Safety." *Camping Magazine* (24 July 1995): 24.

Hammond, Patricia. "Dispelling Myths About Accreditation." *Christian Camp and Conference Journal*. 1997. http://cci.gospelcom.net/ccihome/PPF/pg/publications/default.asp.

Hannah, Nancy and Thomas Berndt. "Relations Between Friendship, Group Acceptance and Evaluations of Summer Camp." *Journal of Early Adolescence* 15, no. 4 (1995): 456–475.

Hirsch, J. "Camp Fatima Priest Allegations Mount." *Foster's Daily Democrat*, 26 May 2002, A1.

Keiser, Susan. "Divorce and Camp: Emotional and Legal Issues." *Camping Magazine* 31 (September 1996).

Kennedy, Richard, and Michael Kimball. *Choosing the Right Camp*. New York: Three Rivers Press, 1996.

Key, Janice. "Illnesses and Injuries at Camp." *Southern Medical Journal* 90, no. 5 (1997): 489–491.

Kong, Delores, and Dan King. "Delores and Dan's Four Thousand Footer Web Site: News About the White Mountains." http://www.geocities.com/fourthousandfooter/news.htm#12/4/00 story.

Lawson, Carol. "Checking Up on Camp Staffs." *New York Times*, 4 July 1996, C1.

Lord, Mary. "Do-Good Camps Attract Teens." *The Boston Globe*, 7 August 2005, B3.

Luciano, Lani. "The Smart Parent's Guide to Choosing a Summer Camp." *Money* (November 1992): 167–175.

Mace, Katherine. "Emergency 911: Putting ACA Standards Into Practice." *Camping Magazine* (May 1998): 48.

Markarian, Marjorie. "Choosing a Summer Camp." *Black Enterprise* (June 1995): 310–312.

National Camp Association. "Guide to Helping Parents Pick the Perfect Camp for Their Child." http://www.summercamp.org/guidance/pamphlet.html.

Pavlicin, Karen. "Embarrassing Situations: Preparing Staff for the

Other Wellness Issues." *Camping Magazine* (May 1997): 6–8.

Rubenstein, Carin. "Worries About Abuse Are Changing Camps." *New York Times,* 9 June 1994, C1, C4.

Rudolf, Mary, Anthony Alario, Brian Youth, and Suzanne Riggs. "Self Medication In Childhood: Observations at a Residential Summer Camp." *Pediatrics* 91, no. 6 (1993): 1182–1185.

Seidman, Anna, and John Patterson. *Kidding Around? A Commitment to Safe Service Opportunities for Young People.* Washington, D.C.: Nonprofit Risk Management Center, 1996.

Shoda, Yuichi, Walter Mischel, and Jack Wright. "The Role of Situational Demands and Cognitive Competencies in Behavior Organization and Personality Coherence." *Journal of Personality and Social Psychology* 65, no. 5 (1993): 1023–1035.

Spears, Gregory. "Serious Summer Camp." *Kiplinger's Magazine* (March 1996): 137–140.

State of Vermont. "Former Camp Director Sentenced for Aggravated Sexual Assault." Press Release. Montpelier, Vt. 20 February 2002. http://www.state. vt.us/atg/press02202002.htm.

Strean, Richard. "Invisible Counselors: Managing What You Don't See." *Camping Magazine* (September 1996): 34–36.

Thompson, Penny, and Nancy Molyneaux. "Enforcing Child Care Standards: Nobody Is Talking About Enforcement: Without It, Standards Are Meaningless." *Public Welfare* 50 (Winter 1992): 20–25.

USA Today. "How to Choose a Summer Camp." (April 1998): 15–16.

VanPelt, Jeffrey. "Amid the Beauty, a Bit of Ugliness." *Fosters Sunday Citizen,* 29 August 1999, A1.

White, Gina. "Camps for Kids: Things to Consider When Selecting a Camp for Your Child." *Equine Journal* (February 2002): 66–70.

Wong, Doris. "More Scrutiny Sought of Summer Camp Staffs." *Boston Globe,* 30 December 1997, A1, A3.

Chapter 9 **Sports** More Than Just a Game

I believe that physical fitness is essential to good health, so I made sure my kids were exposed to many different kinds of athletic activities. Over the years, I learned a lot about children's sports. When the kids were little they had swimming lessons and gymnastics; as they got older they played hockey and soccer and were Little Leaguers. Later they took up tap and ballet, horseback riding, ice-skating, belly-dancing, bowling, tennis, racket ball, and aerial skills like trapeze. We bicycled, jogged, walked, and purchased gym memberships. They liked using their bodies, and they found the activities enjoyable. What they didn't like about sports was the competition, which was injected into the activities not just by coaches, but also by parents and other children. Overzealous encouragement resulted in their discouragement. Pressure to practice became burdensome, and my young athletes found themselves alienated by coaches for not spending virtually all of their discretionary time on the sport. "How can you become any good if you're not willing to put in the necessary effort?" The competitive emphasis pushed by well-meaning adults had a definite impact—the kids quit. Sports were not fun. They felt that they were bad at sports because they weren't quick, adept, or obsessed enough. My children played for recreation, to be with other kids, and to become fit; but other kids played to win, and success and achievement became their sole goal. The sports my children continue now emphasize health and personal achievement, not winning or group bonding.

Sports give children opportunities to learn the values of determination, commitment, hard work, and empathy while acquiring increased self-confidence and positive character traits. Kids who are physically fit are less likely to be obese and have greater energy and aerobic capacity, more efficient respiratory and cardiovascular systems, increased muscle development, and better overall health. Healthy kids also experience social and psychological benefits from being involved in sports. Active children tend to have higher grades, less substance abuse, fewer behavior problems, better school attendance, and a greater ability to work as a team member.

Yet each sport puts young athletes in different kinds of risk. The risk of injury is proportionate to the skill of the children, their training, coaching, supervision, and their appropriate use of quality equipment. For instance, most baseball injuries occur when players slide into base, resulting in over $2 billion in medical costs each year. More than 448,000 football-related injuries to young players cost $7 billion per year, and over 67,000 hockey-related injuries to youths under age fifteen are treated by medical personnel for a cost of $900 million annually. Each year, almost 150,000 young swimmers require medical treatment while 42,000 skiing-related injuries to youths under age fifteen are treated in hospital emergency rooms at a cost of $710 million. Spinal injuries are common among gymnasts, with most occurring during floor exercises, tumbling, or upsets on the balance beam or uneven parallel bars. Equestrian sports are far from risk-free for the quarter million youth involved in 4-H horse and pony programs and the 4.3 million people involved with recreational riding. Because of the variety of risks that exist, parents are advised to find out what kinds of injury rates exist before their children begin a sport.

Soccer is one of the most popular youth sports, and players often suffer bruises and knee, ankle, and shin injuries. The most serious injuries result from heading the ball; cognitive defects, vision problems, and headaches are common in children who use their head to hit the ball. Research has found a link between neurological impairment and head injuries in children, and some physicians believe that heading may cause permanent injury when the brain collides with the skull and becomes bruised. While the American Youth Soccer Organization, an organization that oversees more than 650,000 players on 50,000 teams, has proposed a rule that would ban heading in games and practices for players under age ten, the proposal has not been implemented.

Cheerleading used to be regarded as a support service for sports like football and basketball, but it is much more than a pom-pom-shaking, rhythmic-chanting group of twirlers at pep rallies. Increasing numbers of boys are cheerleaders in this challenging, competitive sport. Over five million cheerleaders spend hours exercising, doing gymnastics, strength training, and challenging physical activities. In the past twenty years, cheerleading accounted for half of the deaths and cases of paralysis among female high school athletes. Ultimate sports, Formula 1 racing–type motorcycle competitions, and skydiving are now marketed to children. Children as young as ten engage in competitive boxing, and there are an estimated 11,000 youth registered as boxers who vie for the National Silver Gloves Tournament.

TYPES OF CHANGES IN YOUTH SPORTS

Sports of today only faintly resemble athletics of the past. Why kids play sports, where they play, what they play with, and who participates has all changed. Over forty million youths participate in sports that are more organized, expensive, and competitive than ever before. While most participate through school-based sports programs, over twenty-five million youth are involved with private or agency-sponsored teams such as Little League Baseball or Pop Warner Football. Over twenty million children play organized out-of-school sports, which are often run by municipal recreation departments in everyone-can-play programs. According to the Sporting Goods Manufacturers Association, over twelve million kids play basketball, seven million play soccer, five million play baseball, and over a half-million kids play hockey. About two million kids pay for private gymnastics, swimming, karate, or skating opportunities.

Social identification.

Sports teams create social cliques that give youth a social network of friends and competitors. Sports teams also provide youth with an identifiable social identity when they wear team clothes or attend sports or social events. As one sixth-grade girl who was not a member of the "in" soccer team told me, "If you're not a Phantom, you're nothing." Children may feel excluded when they're not involved in a sports team that brings attention and prestige to its members. Sports team apparel has become a visible message of a child's interests, associations, and alignments. Million-dollar athletes are promoted as role models.

Parental involvement.

One of the biggest changes in youth sporting activities is the increased involvement of parents. Grandfathers and dads may recall riding their bike to a nearby field to play ball with neighborhood kids. They used simple equipment, made their own rules, and solved their own problems. They tended not to play so long or hard that they got hurt. Their parents didn't organize games or come to watch. Today, parents are so involved that sports are no longer a kid's activity. Highly organized leagues may operate year-round in elaborate facilities. The equipment needed is more sophisticated and expensive. It costs around $500 just to outfit a young hockey player, not counting ice time, lessons, and travel. If parents want their kids to play sports, they drive many miles to multiple practices and games every week. For instance, hockey practices are often timed early in the morning or late at night, and basketball and football games may occur far from home. The schedule, costs, and travel require that parents be involved. Because many parents' work schedules don't allow them to attend all events, other parents take up the slack by driving and watching other people's kids at sporting events. The stakes in kid sports have been raised dramatically, and kids have gotten caught up in the enthusiasm of adults who re-live their sports lives through them. According to Bernard Beck, a Northwestern University sociologist, children learn the same goal-oriented values of competition through sports that their parents have in their careers. Leonard Zaichowsky, professor of sports psychology at Boston University, observes that parental overinvolvement in youth sports has made parental investment higher, increased the stakes, and caused adult behavior to become more out of control as a result. Parents push their own kids to gain skills that will make them better than other players. Kids may be friends at school, but they are encouraged to become competitors on the field. More parents want their kids to have the prestige that comes from playing with the best, which means winning teams, private lessons and trainers, and pushing promising young athletes harder than is wise. Adult coaches, referees, volunteers, and spectators all influence the environment of youth sports.

Coaching style.

Coaches may be judged on whether they produce a winning season, not based on their interpersonal or caregiving skills. The new culture of youth sports encourages competition and a win-at-all-costs attitude. The pressures adults place on kids are so significant that some adults go so far as to teach kids to cheat in order to win. Use of steroid drugs is one form of cheating, and another more commonly used form is lying about the player's age or background; adult sponsors lied about Danny Almonte's age so he could pitch his Little League team into the World Series.

Vehicle to success.

Many youngsters are encouraged to pursue sports early in hopes of getting college scholarships or invitations to join professional teams. While most kids quit playing competitive sports during high school, those who continue want more than a trophy or post-game ice cream. College recruiters flock to high schools and entice prospective recruits with scholarships and new cars. Financially-strapped students who want to go to college may compete for sports scholarships. Wealthy parents may send their kids to expensive sports camps to improve their skills, or they may hire organizations like Grand Slam to get specialized coaching or buy private training sessions for seventy dollars an hour or more. Frenetic competition is now an essential part of sports, even for preschoolers, as child athletes—like Serena and Venus Williams—may be groomed at early ages for college athletics scholarships or a shot on an Olympics team. If children wait until they are older to pursue a sport, it is often too late. Children who are trained when they are young have better chances to become top athletes, while those who are not find it hard to catch up.

NEGATIVE OUTCOMES OF SPORTS INVOLVEMENT

Sports are supposed to be a source of fun and fitness for children, but for many the opposite has occurred. Poor supervision, inadequate handling of crises, lack of equipment, and the inability of adults to control their temper interfere with children's well-being on the field. Many are physically or psychologically abused by adults who are supposed to be watching out for them.

Humiliation and embarrassment.

A normal, human mistake such as making a bad pass or missing a shot at the wrong time can have lifelong consequences. Sports psychologist Shane Murphy says even star athletes buckle under ever-mounting pressure. All too often parents force kids to play when they don't want to, especially if they have made significant financial and emotional investments. Experts believe the most common form of maltreatment in youth sports is emotional abuse. The benefits of sports are so well ingrained in our social consciousness that people have been slow to accept that involvement in sports can traumatize kids. A Minnesota Amateur Sports Commission survey found that almost half of both male and female athletes said they had been called names, yelled at, or insulted, as well as being hit, kicked, or slapped while participating in sports. Emphasis on competition rewards those who are winners; conversely, those who do not win end up feeling like losers. No one, at any age, wants to be considered a failure. It is especially difficult on children because status and acceptance mean a great deal at this developmental stage.

Rejection of sports.

The physical, emotional, and social pressures placed upon young athletes are so great that most decide to quit playing sports. Over three-fourths of the twenty million youth who play organized sports drop out, according to a study by Michigan State University. They drop out because it ceases to be fun and the pressures put on them by coaches and parents don't make it worthwhile, according to Fred Engh, president of the National Alliance for Youth Sports and author of *Why Johnny Hates Sports*. In middle school, informal sports get replaced with competitive, invitational sports. Kids who were active in sports during their elementary school years become disenchanted with sports. Some of this high drop-out rate may be due to busy schedules or sports-related expenses, but much of it is due to children becoming disheartened by the experience. Many find themselves sitting on the sidelines watching the best athletes play. Opponents who are bigger, stronger, and more tenacious quickly erode confidence. It takes courage for a child to get up in front of parents, coaches, and the community to play, and they may be shamed, embarrassed, and ridiculed when they're not as good as others. When winning is the goal, sportsmanship, self-esteem, and interest in athletics fall to the wayside.

Inappropriate parent behavior.

Parents' enthusiasm and support for their young athletes is admirable, but some cross the line into competition, aggression, and violence at sporting events. In Revere, Massachusetts, children watched spectator Thomas Junta kill referee Michael Costin at their hockey practice because he disagreed with Costin's interpretation of a play. The father of a player broke the jaw of a thirteen-year-old umpire at a Little League game in Davie, Florida, because he didn't like the call; a nine-year-old girl in Co Rivera, California, was seriously hurt after twenty-five parents and kids ended up in a brawl after a youth football game; in Illinois a coach was fired after she brandished a meat cleaver during an argument at a junior high volleyball game; and a Virginia mother slapped a fourteen-year-old official at a soccer game and knocked him to the ground because she disagreed with his decision. William Pollack, psychiatry professor at Harvard Medical School, reports that assaults by parents at youth sports events have gotten much worse in the last decade, especially when parents encourage their children to play more aggressively. It has gotten so bad that some parents have been banned from attending sports events. Some schools now require that parents take classes on sportsmanship before they are allowed to attend games.

Sexual abuse.

Young athletes may find themselves sexually abused and harassed both by coaches and teammates. Todd Crosset, professor in sports management at the University of Massachusetts, alleges that some adults who work with young athletes appear charming and helpful on the surface, but sexually abuse the children they coach. When internationally respected hockey coach Graham James was charged with over 350 counts of sexual abuse, the sports community had to consider whether sexual abuse may be more common than expected. Children may be at risk for sexual abuse in three common sporting situations: when they're at overnight sport events, when they are with more-powerful teammates and there is no adult supervision present, and when they spend time alone with coaches or other adults. In most situations where young athletes are sexually abused, the abuse could have been avoided if adults had created better measures for protection. Abuse may be buried or denied when coaches are regarded as godlike figures who are above human weaknesses. Also, coaches hold all the cards over a young athlete's future. The victim and his teammates may keep quiet because the repercussions from exposing the abuse may hinder their future careers.

Steroid use and eating disorders.

An estimated half-million kids in the United States use black-market anabolic steroids to improve athletic performance. Steroids increase body mass and are associated with a host of physical complications, some which can be life-threatening. Other young athletes have serious eating disorders from pressure to cut weight. Steroid use and eating disorders have been found in athletes as young as eleven years old, often without their parents realizing it.

Physical injury.

Sports injuries have reached epidemic proportions in recent years and are the most frequent cause of injury for both male and female adolescents. The types of injuries reflect the increased emphasis on competition and winning. Children's bodies are growing, and bones, tendons, muscles, ligaments, growth plates, and joints can suffer permanent damage if injured during critical stages of development. Between three and five million children are seen in hospital emergency rooms yearly because of sports injuries; eight million more are treated by family physicians for some form of medical problem traceable to athletics. Most of the injuries are preventable and a direct result of pressure on children from parents and coaches to win, according to the National Youth Sports Safety Foundation and the Consumer Product Safety Commission. While injuries during organized sporting events occur, the majority result from informal types of sporting activities in which kids receive less-skilled supervision and coaching. Most injuries occur during practices rather than in games. Most injuries are from football, basketball, baseball, or soccer, since contact sports are the most dangerous for kids. Injuries are likely to result when children don't wear equipment that fits them well, but even when proper equipment is worn and athletes receive training, serious injuries to necks, spinal cords, and growth plates can occur. The most common causes of injuries are falls and being struck by or against objects. Most sports-related injuries in children are soft-tissue injuries including sprains, strains, bruises, and tears. Only about 15 percent of sports injuries involve broken bones; many involve growth-site injuries near the bone where cartilage-like cells will harden and eventually make-up bone mass. This is a vulnerable area of the skeleton that is prone to injury, especially in young adolescents. If growth-site injuries are not diagnosed accurately and treated properly, they can lead to chronic pain, traumatic arthritis, and—in the worse case scenario—deformity and stunted bone growth.

What are the conditioning and training opportunities for young athletes? Each sport emphasizes use of particular body parts, and kids need to slowly build up their muscles, cardiovascular, and respiratory systems to avoid injury. Good trainers and conditioning programs are just as important for young athletes as they are for the pros. Find out what is expected of your child physically at practice, and make sure your child is in the proper physical condition before starting. Advise your child to avoid permanent injury by refusing to play when in pain, and watch how supportive or pushy coaches are at those times.

Some young athletes are asked to perform stunts that aren't really necessary but are appealing to the audience. This includes fancy lifts done by cheerleaders. Cheerleading has become a vigorous sport that includes hurling teammates high into the air. Cheerleaders poised at the top of high pyramids or thrown into the air to perform somersaults are at most risk. While studies on soccer, such as one conducted at Duke University, indicate that heading in soccer may not be dangerous when it is done properly, other experts assert that heading increases the risk of injury. While the crowd may be entertained by such stunts, if risk is associated with a nonessential act, why do it?

While some injuries occur as a result of a sudden impact or fall, others occur slowly from overuse. Nearly half of all sports-related injuries in children are due to overuse or overtraining. Injuries such as teenager's knee, Little League elbow, swimmer's shoulder, and gymnast's back are becoming much more common than in the past. Sports-medicine experts attribute the rise of overuse injuries to the growth of organized sports for kids, early specialization, and sports with year-round seasons. Children are especially vulnerable to overuse injuries because their bones are growing. Years ago there were few overuse injuries because kids controlled their play and played many different games; today sports bureaucracies have emerged, and players extend to the point of discomfort, which they wouldn't do if they were playing on their own. A study by the Minnesota Amateur Sports Commission reported that a quarter of kids have been pressured to play with an injury, which could lead to lifelong problems. Organized sports have a 20 percent re-injury rate that is attributed to inadequate rehabilitation and playing too soon. Adults who do not know enough about how the body works or who put winning ahead of allowing the body to heal have been found to be the central cause of overuse injuries in children.

Some young athletes are encouraged to get back into play before their bodies are fully healed from an injury. This may especially be the case when the team "needs" the injured player to play so that they can win a game. However, there are both short- and long-term problems associated with not letting young athletes heal fully before they go back to play. For instance, studies on osteoarthritis, which affects approximately twenty-one million people, found that a single knee injury early in life can put a person at five times the risk for osteoarthritis in adulthood; likewise a hip injury could more than triple the risk.

Death.

Most sports injuries and deaths are unexpected accidents, such as when seven-year-old Nader Parman of Marietta, Georgia, died of cardiac arrest when a neighbor accidentally hit a line drive into the boy's chest while they played baseball or when Durham, New Hampshire, high school baseball player Matt Sarno died unexpectedly from undiagnosed leukemia. Sports may exacerbate serious health problems and lead to unexpected death, as it did for young athlete Danielle Harman of Stratham, New Hampshire, who complained she didn't feel well and minutes later lay dead on the soccer field.

HOW TO CHOOSE A SAFE SPORT

Decide if you approve of the team's philosophy.

What is the philosophy of the team or sports group? Athletic organizations and specific coaches have their own ideas about how they want to run their programs. There is a huge difference between competitive and cooperative credos.

Identify the right—and wrong—sport for your child.

Is your child ready for the sport? Not every child can do every sport well. Sometimes children are pushed into particular sports prematurely by parents or peers. Children will enjoy the sports more, and do better at them, when they choose their own activities. Participating in different sports can encourage a wider range of skills and body development. Specialization may result in overuse of certain muscles, while participating in multiple physical activities will encourage the development of new skills and physical development.

Get your child a physical examination.

The American Academy of Pediatrics recommends that all children have a pre-sport physical to make sure they are physically able to participate. Researchers have found that as many as half of young athletes do not know how to catch, throw, or hit a ball. Children may have asthma or other health conditions that become exacerbated from exercise. They may have undiagnosed health problems. Parents like to believe that their children are healthy enough for any sports challenge, but they may have genetic, developmental, or acquired problems that may limit their ability to perform certain sports.

Learn and ask questions!

Parents are advised to be partners in their children's sports endeavors. Before children play competitive team sports, ask questions about the coach's training, experience, and philosophy. Find out if there are coaching assistants present. Learn details about the transportation for away games and how overnight accommodations will be handled. Make sure the coach has important health and family information on record for your child.

Use proper safety equipment.

Sometimes players use bats or equipment that are too large for young players to adequately manage. The number of baseball-related injuries could be drastically decreased by the installation of breakaway bases on playing fields. Mouth guards, helmets, chest protectors, and face protectors should be used by young players whenever they play. Many young athletes are not properly attired for the sports in which they participate. Sometimes equipment is used during formal sporting events but not during practices, when harm is just as likely to occur. Even sports like paintball require appropriate protective gear. A father, Kip LaShoto, started a national campaign to promote the use of protective equipment—from Little League games to the PGA Golf Tour—after his son was injured during warm-ups at a Little League game. A ball traveling at 120 miles per hour can cause fractures or serious injuries for children who get hit. LaShoto advocates a law requiring children to wear body armor—such as shatterproof glasses, dentist-fitted mouthpieces, special sun-blocking shirts, athletic supporters, and vests that would protect the area from a child's larynx to his coccyx to keep safe when they play sports like Little League baseball. LaShoto focuses on prevention, but safeguards in children's sports have often resulted from someone getting hurt, according to Richard Lapchick, director of Northeastern University's Center for the Study of Sports.

Find a good coach.

Over four million coaches work with over forty million young athletes in the United States, and while some of them are very competent, others have little or no training. Some are positive role models and others are not. Youth coaches may blindly emulate the win-at-all-cost mentality that filters down from the professional sports entertainment business. Most coaches have no formal training; an estimated 90 percent of youth coaches in the United States have never taken classes designed to enhance their knowledge of the sport they're coaching. Many are unfamiliar with principles of effective motivation and age-appropriate teaching strategies. No certification or accreditation agency exists for youth coaches, and too few education programs for coaches exist. The National Association of Sports Officials shows that 90 percent of state-level sports leaders reported a shortage of coaches and officials, making most youth sports organizations grateful for any help volunteers offer. Some coaches instill high values and empowerment, while others have a win-at-all-cost attitude, which could have negative repercussions. Parents should observe the ways coaches interact with their players, and how they encourage their team to interact with members of the opposing team.

Have an emergency medical assistance plan.

Children routinely get hurt when they play sports and may need immediate medical attention. This means that a CPR-trained coach or adult must be present at all practices and games with a first aid kit and ice packs. There must be a working cell phone available that has pre-programmed numbers for the ambulance, hospital, and physicians. A driver should know the way to the nearest hospital. Because parents may not be present during sporting events, they should have signed release forms so other adults have the authorization to obtain medical care for injured children.

Watch where you sit or stand.

Just watching live sports has become dangerous for children in the stands. The most dangerous seats at baseball games are those behind and near the dugouts because there is no netting in front of them. Fans seated along the third base line must be alert when right-handed power pitchers face left-handed hitters, who are apt to foul the ball into that area. Baseballs can whiz by at one hundred miles per hour. The Baseball Hall of Fame records show at least five deaths of spectators struck by batted or thrown balls, including fourteen-year-old Alan Fish, who died after being hit in the head by a foul ball at a Los Angeles Dodgers' game.

On average, a dozen pucks fly into the seats during every NHL game. Bigger, stronger players and carbon-fiber sticks increase the velocity of six-ounce vulcanized rubber pucks flying through the air, so fans behind the goals are at increased risk of injury. An average of two hundred NHL fans are injured by pucks each season, but this figure may be a gross underestimate, according Dr. Dave Mizman, who gave a paper to the Society for Academic Emergency Medicine on the rising number of spectator hockey injuries. A hockey puck struck thirteen-year-old Brittanie Cecil in the forehead at a Blue Jackets game, causing a skull fracture and bruising of the brain, which led to her death. When attending games, parents are advised to sit children behind protective nets or plexiglass panels to protect them from pucks, balls, or bats traveling into the stands at high speeds. Most of Europe has installed see-through safety nets at many of their sports arenas in order to keep objects from accidentally harming viewers, but this has been opposed in the United States for aesthetic and financial reasons.

Assess training and competence of coaches.

Certified coaches are much safer than coaches who haven't been trained to prevent injuries. When there are standards and guidelines in place to prevent possible problems, young athletes and spectators are protected. The public has been slow to demand regulation for coaches and ensure proper safeguards for young athletes. The University of New Hampshire's gymnastics youth program demonstrates how good coaching and skills training can help children enjoy sports in a safe and responsible way. Coaches Gail Goodspeed and Ed Datti have created a philosophy and set of practices that preserve individual integrity while promoting healthy, fun sports education for children as young as kindergarteners. The quality of coaching can make or break a child, so it's important to find the good ones and avoid the others. Danger occurs when parents or coaches live through the children, according to Ronald Smith, a psychologist at the University of Washington. These people push children too hard while trying to live vicariously through them. The need to win has resulted in coaches allowing players to play too rough; Minnesota researchers found that body checking accounted for 59 percent of hockey injuries (20 percent from legal checking and 39 percent from illegal checking) and that coach-oriented rules violations were responsible for another 27 percent.

PROMISING PROGRAMS

The sports community appears to recognize that it has a multifaceted problem with child safety, and segments of it are actively striving to make sports safer. The National Alliance for Youth Sports, a nonprofit group whose mission is to promote sports as a vehicle for developing character and values, was started in 1981 when its founders felt child sports had become too competitive and discouraging. At one time children played games for fun in a healthy atmosphere of support and encouragement, but championships, all-star teams, cheating, and playing when injured give young athletes the wrong messages, according its founder, Fred Engh. The National Summit on Raising Community Standards in Children's Sports addresses the problem of violence and declining levels of sportsmanship in athletic programs. Recreation and youth-sports professionals from around the country have begun to network together to develop standards to help improve the environment of youth sports. Much of their work is centered on how to better educate coaches and parents about acceptable behavior. Northeastern University's Center for the Study of Sport, the National Institute for Child Centered Coaching in Utah, and the Institute for the Study of Youth Sports at Michigan State University are helping to increase awareness of sports and their relation to society. They have developed programs that identify problems, offer solutions, and promote the benefits of sports. Pediatricians and orthopedic physicians are working together to better understand children's sports injuries and develop prevention strategies. Because of gaps in coaching quality, a variety of groups have begun to improve coaching standards and playing conditions for young players. While the multibillion-dollar professional sports industry is an entertainment business, youth athletics is by its very nature an educational activity, according to Stanford University's Positive Coaching Alliance. Coaches are encouraged to focus on how they teach game rules, strategies, skills, discipline, teamwork, and cooperation, since these are messages that get lost in the win-at-all-costs mentality so prevalent in youth sports. The alliance seeks to reduce parents and coaches who scream on the sidelines, since they're obviously not thinking about the child's development. The Amateur Athletic Union has established a youth athletics program that coaches, volunteers, officials, and athletes can join. They're putting "very tough" procedures in place to document that all their clubs, coaches, and athletes are properly registered before allowing them to compete. The Parents Association for Youth Sports (PAYS) teaches parents about the importance of sportsmanship at their children's athletic events. PAYS programs have been used in almost three hundred cities nationwide. See appendix A for details about a code of conduct for adults working with young athletes.

RESOURCES

American Association for
Horsemanship Safety
PO Box 39
Fentress, TX 78622
(512) 488-2220

American Association of Cheerleading
6745 Lenox Center Court, Suite 318
Memphis, TN 38115
(800) 533-6583
http://www.aacca.org

American Red Cross
2025 E Street, NW
Washington, DC 20006
(202) 303-4498
http://www.redcross.org

American Youth Soccer Organization
AYSO National Support and Training
Center
12501 S. Isis Ave.
Hawthorne, CA 90250
http://soccer.org

Sports Safety: Injury Statistics and
Incidence Rates
http://www.childrenshospital.org/az/
Site1110/mainpageS1110P0.html

Carnegie Foundation
The Role of Sports in Youth Development
51 Vista Lane
Stanford, CA 94305
(650) 566-5100
http://www.carnegie.org/reports/
poinst1.htm

Center for the Study of Sport in Society
Northeastern University
Boston, MA 02115-5000
(617) 373-4025
http://www.sportinsociety.org

Institute for the Study of Youth Sports
Michigan State University
IM Sports Circle, 201
East Lansing, MI 48824
http://www.msu.edu

Kids Sports Network
8206 Roughrider, Suite 104
San Antonio, TX 78239
(210) 654-4707
http://www.ksnusa.org/childcentered.
htm

Medline Plus
Sports Safety
8600 Rockville Pike
Bethesda, MD 20894
(888) 346-3656
http://www.nlm.nih.gov/medlineplus/
sportssafety.html

Minnesota Amateur Sports Commission
1700 105th Ave., NE
Blaine, MN 55449
(763) 785-5630
http://www.mnsports.org

National Alliance for Youth Sports
2050 Vista Parkway
West Palm Beach, FL 33411
(800) 729-2057
http://www.NAYS.org

National Association of Sports Officials
2017 Lathrop Ave.
Racine, WI 53405
(262) 632-5448
http://www.naso.org

National Youth Sports Safety Foundation
One Beacon Street, Suite 3333
Boston, MA 02108
(617) 367-6677
http://www.nyssf.org

Ozark Orthopedic
Youth and Sports
Highway 14E
Mountain View, AR 72560
(870) 269-8300
http://www.ozarkortho.com/patiented/
youth.htm

Positive Coaching Alliance
Department of Athletics
Arrilaga Family Sports Center
Stanford University
Stanford, CA 94305-6150
http://www.positivecoach.org

Safe Kids USA
1301 Pennsylvania Ave., NW
Suite 1000
Washington, DC 20004-1707
http://www.usa.safekids.org

Safer Child, Inc.
General Sports Safety for Children
PO Box 47151
Spokane, WA 99228-1151
http://www.saferchild.org/general3.htm

Sporting Goods Manufacturers
Association
1150 17th St., NW, #850
Washington, DC 20036
(202) 775-1762
http://www.sgma.com

Sports Safety
University of Michigan Health System
1500 E. Medical Center Drive
Ann Arbor, MI 48109
(734) 936-4000
http://www.med.umich.edu/1libr/
yourchild/sportsaf.htm

REFERENCES

Abel, David. "Playing It Safe," *Boston Globe*, 27 July 2001, B1.

Abraham, Yvonne. "Weymouth Soccer Coach Faces New Assault Charge," *Boston Globe*, 14 March 1999, B5.

"Adults, Kids, Brawl at Football Game." *CNN*, 18 October 2002. http://www.cnn.com.

Arthritis Foundation. *"Safe or Sorry: A Parent's Guide to Sports Injury Prevention."* http://www.arthritis.org/resources/SIP/intro.asp.

Axtman, Chris. "Extreme Cheerleading: How Schools Grapple with the New Risks." *Christian Science Monitor*, 24 June 2004. http://www.csmonitor.com/2004/0624/p01s01-usgn.html.

Beck, Bernard. "Youth Sports." Northwestern University. 2004. http://www.sociology.northwestern.edu/faculty/cv/cvbeck.pdf.

Blade's On Ice. *"Sexual Abuse in Sports."* Professional Skater's Association. http://www.silent-edge.org/survey.html. 1999.

Brust J., Barbara Leonard, and A. Pheley. "Children's Ice Hockey Injuries". *American Journal of Disabled Children* 146, no. 6 (1992):741–747.

Burke, E., and D. Kleiber. "Psychological and Physical Implications of Highly Competitive Sports for Children." In *Sport Psychology,* edited by W. Straub: 305–313. Ithaca N.Y.: Movement Publications, 1980.

Butterfield, Fox. "A Fatality, Parental Violence and Youth Sports." *New York Times,* 11 July 2000, A14.

Cable News Network. "'Hockey Dad' Gets 6 to 10 Years for Fatal Beating." *CNN,* 25 January 2002. http://archives.cnn.com/2002/LAW/01/25/hockey.death.verdict/index.html.

Cafardo, Nick. "Boyd Denies Ex-Clubhouse Kids' Drug Allegations." *Boston Globe,* 22 May 2002, B4.

CBS News. "Girl Killed by Stray Hockey Puck." Columbus, Ohio. 20 March 2002. http://www.cbsnews.com.

Chandler, Gary. "Invitational Practices in Middle School Athletics." *Journal of Invitational Theory and Practice* 4, no. 1 (1966): 37–56.

Duda, J. "Consider the Children: Meeting Participants Goals in Youth Sports." *Journal of Physical Education, Recreation and Dance* 56 (1985): 55–56.

Duff, John F. *Youth Sports Injuries.* New York: Macmillan, 1992.

Eason, Kevin. "Lure of Cash Means Track Rage Is Rife at Go-Kart Circuits." *The Times Sports Daily,* 30 October 2001, 1.

Engh, Fred. *Why Johnny Hates Sports.* New York: Avery Publishing Group, 1999.

Farber, Michael. "Put Up the Net: Spectators Don't Want Their Views Obstructed, but Protecting Fans, as European Leagues Do, Should Be an NHL Priority." *Sports Illustrated* (1 April 2002): 62–65.

Flegel, Melinda. "Sports First Aid." *Human Kinetics* (1992): 18–19.

Foster's Daily Democrat. "Students Humiliated, Beaten to Join Groups." 29 August 2000, B14

"Foul Play! Parents and Coaches Can Save Sportsmanship From Extinction." *Sports Parents Magazine.* Youth Sports Report, 2004: 26.

Gaines, Susan. "Child's Play? Kids, Sports, and Injury." *Minnesota Medical Association* 83 (June 2000).

Gehring, John. "More Schools Call Foul on Unsportsmanship Like Behavior." *Education Week* (17 October 2001). http://www.edweek.org/ew/newstory.cfm?slug=07parents.h21.

Girls' and Women's Sport Institute. "What Is Child Maltreatment in Youth Sports?" 2005. http://www.masc.state.mn.us/resources/kyss&f/brochure3.htm.

Hines, S., and D. Groves. "Sports Competition and Its Influence On Self-Esteem Development." *Adolescence* 24, no. 96 (1989): 861–869.

Kirshnit, C., B. Harn, and N. Richards. "The Sporting Life: Athletic Activities During Early Adolescence." *Journal of Youth and Adolescence* 18, no. 6 (1989): 601–615.

Landers, Ann. "Parents Should Trust Their

Gut Feelings." *Foster's Daily Democrat,* 30 April 2001, 6B.

———. "Pushy Parents Can Cause Harm." *Foster's Daily Democrat,* 25 November 2001, 2E.

McGregor, Marg. "What Parents Can Do About Harassment and Abuse in Sport." Canadian Association for Women and Sport and Physical Activity. 2005. http://www.harassmentinsport.com/e/parents/index.htm#safe.

Micheli, Lyle J. *Sportswise: An Essential Guide for Young Athletes, Parents, and Coaches.* Boston: Houghton Mifflin, 1990.

National PTA. "Children, Sports and Injuries—What Parents Ought to Know." *National PTA Health and Safety Update.* Chicago, Ill.: National PTA, 1994.

Poinsett, Alex. "The Role of Sports in Youth Development." Report for Carnegie Corporation of New York. 18 March 1996.

Portsmouth Herald. "Danielle Harman." Obituary. 29 April 1995, A26.

Remak, B. "Starting Them Right: Helping Parents to Prepare Young Children For Sports." *Strategies* 2, no. 1 (1988): 14–16.

Reppucci, N. Dickon. "Prevention and Ecology: Teen Pregnancy, Child Sexual Abuse, and Organized Youth Sports." *American Journal of Community Psychology* 15 (February 1987): 1–22.

Riernicke, C. "All Must Play—The Only Way for Middle School Athletics." *Journal of*

Physical Education, Recreation and Dance 59 (1988): 82–84.

Slade, Sean. "How Do Athletics Affect Us in the Long Run?" *The Journal of Physical Education, Recreation, and Dance* (March 1999): 37–39.

Smith, Stephen. "Cheerleaders Given an A for Accidents." *Boston Globe,* 22 October 2002, A5.

Smoll, Frank, and Ronald Smith. *Sports and Your Child: A 50 Minute Guide for Parents.* University of Washington. Portola Valley, Calif.: Warde Publishers, Inc. 2002.

Spindt, G. B. "Athletics for Everyone." *Journal of Physical Education, Recreation and Dance* 55 (1984): 47.

Stankovich, Christopher E., and Todd M. Kays. "The Parent's Playbook: Developing a Game Plan for Maximizing Your Child's Athletic Experience." July 2002. http://www.championathletic.com/testimonials/products.htm.

Stephens, Dawn. "Aggressive Behavior in Girl's Sports." *International Journal of Sport Psychology* (December 1997).

Swarbrick, Jack. "USA Gymnastics Code of Ethics: Sexual Misconduct." *Womensport* 2, no. 3 (1997).

Tator, C.H., V. E. Edmonds, L. Lapczak, et al. "Spinal Injuries in Ice Hockey Players, 1966–1987." *Canadian Journal of Surgery* 34, no. 1 (1991): 63–69.

Trocci, Mike, and John Doyle. "Oyster River Junior Athlete Sarno Dies of Leukemia."

http://orhs2004.tripod.com/news/ matt percent20sarno2.htm.

Tufts University. "Nader Parman of Marietta, Georgia Killed in Heartbreaking Baseball Accident." *Tufts E-News.* 2002. http://www.tufts. edu/communications/stories/ 052202Heartbreaking.htm.

Silent Edge: Advocacy for Skaters. "The Sheldon Kennedy/Graham James Case: Sexual Abuse in Canadian Junior Hockey." Reprint from *Atlanta Journal-Constitution,* 17 January 1999. http://www.silent-edge.org/kennedy. html.

United States Gymnastics Federation. *Child Abuse in Youth Sports.* Indianapolis, Ind.: United States Gymnastics Federation, 2004.

Vaszily, Brian. "Cheerleading: Becoming as Dangerous as These Top 7 Most Dangerous Youth Sports?" 2006. http://ezinearticles. com/?Cheerleading:-Becoming-as-Dangerous-As-These-Top-7-Most-Dangerous-Youth-Sports?&id=127767.

Wong, Edward. "Concerns About Heading by Youth Soccer Players Set Off Debate." *New York Times,* 25 November 2001, 8:1.

Chapter 10 Transportation Safety

Church school bus driver Otto Nuss picked up thirteen children, ages six through fifteen, for their daily 6-mile trip to school in Birdsboro, Pennsylvania, but when the bus did not arrive at its destination, parents and teachers knew something was wrong. Without authorization, Nuss had decided to take the children on a 115-mile trip to Washington, D.C. An avid gun collector, Nuss, who had passed criminal background and child abuse checks, had a loaded Springfield M-1 rifle behind his drivers' seat on the bus. The children reportedly had a good time on the trip; he took them to Burger King for lunch en route. Only after Nuss was apprehended did the children realize the gravity of the situation. Nuss reportedly had a history of psychiatric problems and had recently gone off his medication.

Aunnalise Woods was on a Los Angeles America West flight to see her father in Detroit. Her mother paid a sixty-dollar fee for an airline chaperone to accompany her daughter on her connecting flight. When Aunnalise didn't arrive, an airline attendant told her father, Bill McDaniel, that his daughter was flying standby and would arrive on a later flight at 10:00 p.m. She wasn't on that flight either. Airline representatives did not know where she was. The airline chaperone had put the child on the wrong flight, and Aunnalise did not realize it until the plane landed in Orlando. She was put on another flight to Detroit—one that connected through Las Vegas—to finally meet her father in Detroit, over eighteen hours after she left Los Angeles.

Are such horror stories unusual or more common than parents would like to think? How safe are children when they are being transported by people other than their parents? Each day, millions of children are placed in the care of other people as they are transported by bus, plane, car, subway, taxi, and van. Transportation is an essential component of caring for children. Kids must be able to get to and from home, school, gym, church, and other activities. Often, organizations provide transportation as part of their services. Parents may contract with individual caregivers to take their kids from one location to another. Children may also ride informally with other parents to sports or recreational activities. Most forms of transportation are assumed to be safe until an accident occurs. When parents consider the realistic risks that children face when they're being transported, they can put into place procedures to prevent future problems.

Transporting children is a particularly difficult problem for caregivers, according to the Nonprofit Risk Management Center. When organizations or individuals assume responsibility for transporting young people, they automatically assume the responsibility of performing this task safely. Sometimes there is an explicit contractual arrangement, such as when Tri Star Gymnastics picks up children from school and takes them to their facility for after-school gymnastics programs or when the public school bus hauls students to an away basketball game. The providers may have their own bus and drivers or contract with a transportation agency responsible for picking up the kids, driving them to their destination, and returning them safely. In these situations, there is a formal agreement for the transport of children, and the organization should have initiated safeguards to prevent problems. They should have vehicles that are inspected and approved for the transportation of children, and they should hire drivers with demonstrated training and competence. The risk is greater when organizations let parents transport other people's children, as often occurs on field trips. Parents who volunteer to drive are too-often assumed to be good drivers with safe vehicles. Most of the time, adults who volunteer to transport children never have their backgrounds checked to determine if they are good drivers and safe to be around children. Parents have no idea if their cars have new or bald tires or if the seat belts work properly. They also have no control over what is talked about when children are en route, what music they listen to, or the behavior of other riders. How can parents reduce the risks when other people transport children?

TYPES OF DRIVERS

Friends and relatives.

Parents routinely rely upon family and friends to take their children places when they cannot. Parents usually know the driving ability of people in their close network. But sometimes they rely upon people they do not know well to transport their children, such as distant friends, acquaintances, or parents or siblings of their children's friends. Sometimes parents may not even know the people who give their children rides. Parents may feel awkward asking people who volunteer to transport their kids about their driving records or if their car is insured and reliable. Usually, parents do not ask such questions and trust that their children will arrive home safely.

Babysitters, au pairs, and nannies.

As employers, parents can request detailed information about the driving record of babysitters, nannies, au pairs, and governesses. If they do not, they play roulette with their children's lives. Confidence that the children are in a safe vehicle can be enhanced when the caregivers drive a car provided by the parents.

Daycare, schools, and child-centered organizations.

Transporting children is a necessary and commonly used service for organizations like schools, daycare centers, and organizations like the YMCA. They usually have their own vehicles and trained drivers or contract with a transportation organization. The more often they provide the service, such as daily bus service to and from public schools, the more likely they are to have instituted a comprehensive transportation plan and policy. When organizations infrequently transport children, they are more likely to do so in haphazard ways.

Volunteers.

Many organizations ask parent volunteers to transport children on field trips or sporting events. Carpooling is a convenient way for parents to get kids where they need to go without being a constant chauffeur. There is a built-in assumption that all parents will be responsible and reliable. However, there is usually no prescreening or follow-up to determine whether this assumption is true. Usually, the only time driver competence is questioned is after an accident occurs. According to risk management organizations, the documented driving competence of volunteers should be the same as for paid employees.

Public transportation operators.

Tens of thousands of public servants are hired each year to transport other people's kids. These include taxi drivers, bus drivers, airline pilots, subway drivers, train engineers, and boat pilots, not to mention all the associated public transportation representatives. Because these people have been hired by official transportation agencies, parents automatically assume that the organizations have done a good job screening applicants and training those who have been hired. They are usually competent drivers. However, parents must realize that they were hired to transport people—not to be babysitters or child monitors. Children who ride in planes, trains, boats, and buses are supposed to be self-contained unless they are with an adult, meaning that they should know how to get on and off the vehicle safely, behave while they are in the vehicle, and get to where they need to go. It is not the responsibility of transportation authorities to escort children unless parents have specifically set up that arrangement, as may occur with airlines. Interpersonal skills may not be important employment skills for those specifically hired to drive large transportation vehicles.

TYPES OF VEHICULAR RISK

The safety of children may vary depending on the kind of vehicle in which they ride:

Automobiles.

Children are most likely to be transported by car. Motor vehicle crashes are the leading cause of death among children in the United States and account for 27 percent of all childhood deaths. Each year they take the lives of around 2,100 child passengers fifteen years and younger and injure another 327,500 severely enough to require emergency treatment. A recent study found that every day an average of 7 children are killed and 866 are injured in auto accidents. Child deaths cluster around two age groups. One group is teen drivers, who are inexperienced and prone to have accidents. The other is children ages four to eight, who are too big for car seats and too little to fit well in seat belts designed for adults, according to the National Highway Traffic Safety Administration. The automobile industry has actively sought to create safer cars through construction design and the implementation of airbags and seat belts. The most likely cause of injuries and deaths are human error and could therefore be prevented.

Buses.

Cars may be the most common type of transportation used by kids, but over half of school-aged children ride school buses on a daily basis, while others ride them for public transportation or special outings. Pupil transportation first began in the late 1800s. The first school buses were horse-drawn carts borrowed from local farmers. They were later replaced with gasoline-powered school trucks. During the 1930s, as the nation's roadways expanded, the need for vehicles to transport schoolchildren grew, which led to the formation of an industry to manufacture buses. Today there are about half a million yellow school buses on the road in the United States transporting twenty-five million children to school. When the daily ridership is multiplied by the number of school days, school buses annually provide rides to ten billion students across five billion miles at a cost of over $10 billion. Most school buses are owned and operated by transportation contractors, local entrepreneurs, nationwide student transportation companies, and school districts. The federal government regulates the bus manufacturing industry with consultation from the National School Transportation Association so that all school buses meet certain safety standards.

How safe are school buses? As the number of school buses on the roads increased, so did injuries and fatalities. This prompted the development of safety guidelines. The National Safety Council reports that today school buses are the safest form of ground transportation, much safer than the family car because they are bigger, heavier, and sit higher off the ground. Their yellow color, flashing lights, and swing-out stop signs make them highly visible to motorists. They must meet rigorous federal standards from fuel-tank protection to seating systems and emergency exits. Drivers are supposed to have commercial driver licenses and specialized training.

Despite these safeguards, school bus safety has regained public attention due to accidents like the one in Kentucky in 1988, when 24 children were killed after a drunk driver hit their bus as they returned home from King's Island Amusement Park. They died not from the impact of the crash, but from being trapped inside during the resulting fire; a guard on the bus's fuel tank had not been installed. School bus accidents have resulted in fatalities in most states, but advocates point out that only 0.3 percent of over 426,000 fatal traffic crashes were school bus related. According to transportation statistics, 11 children die each year in school bus crashes, compared with over 8,000 who die in all other types of motor vehicle accidents. But critics say that since 1985, over 1,500 children have died in school bus related crashes, an average of 134 fatalities per year, or an increase of 94 percent.

Human error can be the cause of injury and fatality. For example, four students from Newton, Massachusetts, died in a bus crash on their way home from a field trip to New Brunswick. The weather was foggy and the accident occurred at 4:15 in the morning, when the tired driver missed an exit. They were traveling through the night because the school did not want to put the children in hotels overnight. In another case of human error, dozens of children were sent to Garland, Texas–area hospitals when the driver lost control of a chartered bus and crashed into a pillar en route to church camp.

Most fatalities do not occur when children are riding in the bus, but when pupils enter or exit the bus. There is a blind spot, called the danger zone area, around the bus when they momentarily become invisible to both the bus driver and approaching motorists. The classic school bus has a large blind-spot area that the driver cannot see, and there have been cases where children were run over by their own bus. Children crossing the street may be hit by motorists who illegally pass a stopped bus, or youngsters may be hit when they dart in front of, next to, behind, or under the bus. While school buses are touted as one of the safest forms of transportation, human error and structural features still impact children's safety in and around the bus.

Airlines.

Children can be put into potentially risky situations when they fly. Risks are particularly significant for children flying alone and babies who ride without being in flight seats. While parents may prefer to keep children under age two on their laps rather than paying additional money for a seat, children are at significant risk if there is turbulence or an accident. Unrestrained babies are known in the airline industry as missiles because they can quickly fly out of parent's arms when the plane unexpectedly shifts and passengers are jostled. The Federal Aviation Administration (FAA) has found most turbulence-related injuries and death occur when the seat belt sign is on and people don't wear them, or when people hold children on their laps to play or look out the window. The National Transportation Safety Board (NTSB) and the Los Angeles Area Child Passenger Safety Association recognize that children's lives should not be dependent upon the strength of their parent's grip, and they have petitioned the FAA to require the use of restraint systems for passengers of all ages. There is currently a proposed airline children's safety bill that would give children under age two the same protection as older passengers. James Kolstand of the NTSB notes that luggage, coffee pots, portable computers, and adult passengers must be secured for takeoff and landing and during turbulence, yet the most precious cargo on the plane, infants and toddlers, are left unrestrained. Even pets have more stringent regulations to ensure their safety than young children. Because the potential for injury in an aircraft flying at 550 miles per hour is much greater than the potential for injury in an automobile traveling at 50 miles per hour, advocates for child safety seats on planes believe restraints could prevent injuries and save young lives.

Most children fly with their parents, but children increasingly fly alone. The Air Transport Association indicates as many as 22,000 children travel alone each day, with most unescorted minors traveling during the summer and school holiday periods. Children may fly alone to visit grandparents or divorced parents, on school trips, or to return home from school. With increasing numbers of flight delays, switching planes at airports, and other airline glitches, sending a child on a plane alone is a source of anxiety for parents, children, and airlines. Children between five and twelve who travel without a parent or guardian are known as "unaccompanied minors." Just because five-year-olds are permitted to fly solo does not mean that they will be able to handle flying alone, especially if they are nervous, have behavioral problems, must make a connection, or have never flown before. Many airlines do not allow children who are under seven to make connections, but when they do, they must be assisted by airline personnel—with an escort fee of around $75 each way to cover costs for transferring the child from plane to plane. Most airlines do not provide escort service to follow children all the way through the process; they only get them from one gate to another. Between the time when children are dropped off at the gate and when it is time to board, they are on their own. While there may be airline representatives working the gate area, they are usually busy checking in passengers, answering questions, corresponding with the cock-pit, and so on. When busy doing their official job, they simply cannot watch over children. If children have to go to the bathroom, no one escorts them down the crowded hallways and into the bathroom, and no one makes sure they get back to the gate area afterwards. No airline official knows if the child stops into a store to look at magazines or buy gum.

Usually parents cannot go into the restricted access areas past the security checkpoint. Parents must be aware that even infants and toddlers may be selected for random screening, so they should teach their children about what to expect and how to behave when they go through security checks. Once through the security checkpoint, the child should be taken to the gate and seated near an airline representative near the gate check-in counter. When time to board the plane, the child is supposed to be escorted for pre-boarding. They are then in the hands of the flight attendants, who vary significantly in their attentiveness to children. Parents are advised to send plenty of water, food, and things for children to do, since unanticipated delays may occur. Once the flight has ended, the child is supposed to sit and wait until everyone is off the plane, whereupon some designated airline person escorts the child off the plane and to the person meeting her. The person doing the pick-up is supposed to show proper identification. Then, the child and escort part company. If this careful orchestration works, the child makes it to her destination safely.

Public transportation and taxis.

In urban areas, children may regularly ride on public transportation vehicles such as subways and buses. Each has its own policies about transporting children, especially those who are alone. In general, public transportation systems allow children of any age to ride so long as they are not causing a disruption. It is not the driver's job to go out of his way to monitor young passengers.

Subway systems generally have no age limitations for how old kids need to be in order to travel on the fast-moving trains. Often, children travel with parents or friends, but many youngsters travel alone to and from school, to meet parents, or for recreation. Children with subway passes can easily slip past officials and get onto any subway. Often there are no subway personnel in the tunnels where trains speed by. Small children waiting too close to the edge could accidentally lose their balance and tumble onto the tracks. Lots of people walk through a subway station within minutes. Kids could become easily lost and are susceptible to interactions with strangers.

Public bus drivers are hired because they are trained to drive large vehicles. They are not hired to be nannies. Unlike the subway, the driver sees every person who gets on the bus, and they can ask kids questions to make sure they know where they are going. If a child is being hassled, stays on the bus too long, or exhibits inappropriate behavior, the driver is present to intercept problems. However, the care they give may be more a product of individual concern than organizational policy.

Taxis are also used for transportation in urban areas. They are private companies that contract with specific patrons to provide a particular service for a designated period of time. As a result, they seem to have more stringent policies about transporting kids than public buses or subways. Because it was difficult to find literature on taxi policies for transporting children, I conducted telephone interviews with two-dozen cab companies across the nation and found that most cab companies will not transport unaccompanied children under the age of twelve, and some want them to be at least sixteen. But how would a worker at the end of a phone know the age of the child calling for a ride? Taxi companies indicate that they ask a series of questions when they are called for a ride, and if the caller appears young they ask more questions. Part of their rigor is to make sure they get paid, since kids may not have cash or credit cards. Another concern is that if anything goes wrong inside the cab, the passenger is usually held responsible, but if the passenger is under fourteen, then the cab company is responsible. Taxis prefer that a responsible adult puts children into the cab and meets them at their destination. If there no adult is waiting, cabs regularly wait with the child until one comes, for both economic and safety reasons. Adolescents over twelve are often supposed to be traveling with someone over age sixteen until they are around that age themselves, but this is difficult to document because kids can look and act much older than they are. If children ride with an older persons, their relationship may not be of concern to the driver, especially if their behavior is appropriate inside the cab. Cab companies do not want to be responsible for problems that could result in transporting young children and may encourage them to use limos instead, since parents can contract with them to transport their children to and from school on a regular basis, pay by credit card, and contract with the limo drivers to be in charge of the kids.

HOW TO CHOOSE SAFE TRANSPORTATION FOR CHILDREN

Children must use transportation provided by people other than parents, and parents don't need to worry about their children's safety if they've done their homework. After all, no situation is entirely risk-free, especially when it comes to transportation accidents, but parents can anticipate that their kids will be safe if they know what to look for.

Make sure children are never left alone in the car.

Children should never be left alone in the car, unattended, even for short periods of time. Some drivers leave kids in the car with the engine running while they go into the store or run errands. Kids alone in cars may be vulnerable to extremes in heat or cold; the inside of a parked car can exceed 122 degrees within fifteen minutes on a typical sunny summer day. Opening the window slightly does not keep the temperature at a safe level. Infants are five times more sensitive to heat than adults, and their small bodies cannot regulate their body temperatures as quickly as adults. Rising temperatures inside a car can cause a child to suffer from heat stress, dehydration, and shock. In Tennessee a driver for Children's Palace left a twenty-two-month-old baby inside a parked van in Memphis for more than seven hours in 90 degree heat. The same day, two-year-old Brandon Mann was left in a van outside Pee Wee Wisdom Learning Center and died. Similarly, children left unattended in cars could freeze quickly if the car is turned off during the winter, or they could accidentally knock the transmission out of park if the engine is on. They could get out of the car and get lost or hit, or they could be abducted. Despite not wanting to awaken a sleeping baby, there is never a reason good enough to leave a young child alone in a car.

Make sure the vehicles are safe.

This is not always possible to do, especially with planes, trains, and subways. But parents can get a pretty good idea if the cars their children may be transported in are safe just by looking at them. For instance, many states require that cars be inspected, and a sticker is visibly placed on the windshield to indicate that a mechanic has checked basic safety features such as tires, brakes, lights, and windshield wiper function. If the car has obvious repairs that have not been made, parents may be rightfully concerned that the driver is not attentive to safety. New vehicles are probably safe, but organizations with pinched budgets are more likely to purchase used vehicles. Older vehicles may be riskier because safety features have changed significantly over time, and many used cars have been driven to death by the time they are sold. School buses are designed with structural integrity, large outside mirrors, emergency exits, warning lights, fuel system integrity, and stop signal arms. The school bus is painted bright yellow in order to be highly visible. The weight, structure, and design of the seats and seat backs provide added safety benefits.

While the use of seat belts is considered a safety feature in cars, parents should realize that it is still a controversial procedure, especially in school buses. There is no federal law requiring seatbelts for full-size school buses, although lap belts are required on smaller-model buses, because the vehicles offer less crash protection than full-size ones. While seat belt legislation was introduced in sixteen states in 1997, to date, it has passed in none. Towns like Calais, Vermont, have taken measures to safeguard their buses, since the federal government gives school districts, towns, and states the right to decide for themselves. Opponents to seatbelts on buses argue that adding them to a sixty-five-passenger bus would cost too much and that children are more often injured outside in loading zones, not inside the bus. They argue that money would be better spent on safety measures such as mirrors, stop-arms, padded high-back seats, and improved driver training. School transportation and National Highway Traffic Safety Administration (NHTSA) officials argue that, if worn incorrectly, one-piece lap belts can cause abdominal or neck injuries in crashes, and that younger, less-dexterous children might not be able to free themselves in an emergency. It is instructive to note that the government, through NHTSA, recommended seat belts in buses back in 1975, but the corporate school bus lobby, the National School Transportation Association, took credit for an expensive lobbying campaign that persuaded NHTSA to back down. Seatbelts on large school buses have been endorsed by the American Medical Association, American Academy of Pediatrics, American Academy of Orthopedic Surgeons, National PTA, Fire Marshals Association, American College of Preventive Medicine, and the National Coalition of School Bus Safety.

Find out if your bus has motion detectors and radar devices, which help drivers sense the presence of a moving object close to the bus (like a child); cameras that monitor blind spots outside the bus; a mechanical crossing-control arm mounted on the bus's front bumper that prevents kids from crossing where the driver cannot see them; and flat-front buses with the engine moved to the back, which allow the driver to see small children near the front bumper. Parents can find out whether a van that is painted to look like a school bus actually has the same type of safety features as real buses. Vans may be used because they are cheaper and can be driven by someone without a commercial license or special training, but most don't conform to federal requirements for school buses, because they do not have emergency exits, extra mirrors, flashing lights, stop-arms, or meet structural standards. Because the law is loosely written, little-known, and laxly enforced, after-school programs, daycare centers, camps, or early-childhood education programs may use vans instead of buses. They simply are not as safe as a bus for the transportation of children.

Prepare children for traveling without you.

Not all children are mature enough to handle traveling alone. Parents should decide if their children are emotionally able to handle traveling without a parent present, if they will behave, and if they will know what to do in case of an emergency. When children travel without parents, it is useful for them to carry personal information, such as their name, age, where they are going, parents' phone numbers, and other relevant information, such as if they have a medical condition for which they may need special care. Children should know how to contact parents by phone and have other people they can contact if they need help. Parents should make sure their children have the resources they need to take care of themselves, such as money, ways to entertain themselves, or packed snacks. Children should be taught how to be safe and appropriate passengers when they are in any form of transportation. If children are on boats, they must know not to engage in horseplay, because someone could slip or fall overboard. If they fight near train tracks, they may accidentally fall and be run over. When they ride the school bus, parents must realize that many students have to sit three-deep in seats that are too narrow for their bodies and possessions; if they are on the subway, they must know how to protect themselves and their belongings. On airplanes, there is a flight attendant whom they can contact; on a train they can contact the conductor. But many trains and subway cars don't have any adult available. Parents need to know if their children are competent enough to get themselves through airports, subway, and train stations; many are complicated and confusing even for adults and challenging to maneuver in a time crunch. Walking children through a trial run will be helpful for both parents and kids and increase the chances for a safe journey.

Anticipate problems.

Parents should anticipate the impact of weather conditions, delays, and the possibility of late or missed connections. Watch the weather. Rain, snow, fog, icy weather, and night driving or congested traffic multiply the risk. Call the airport to make sure planes are on schedule. Reports indicate that one in four flights are delayed. According to the Department of Transportation's air travel consumer report for July 2001, Southwest Airlines operated 31 flights (out of nearly 2,800 total) that were late 70 percent of the time or more that month. Some flights may be delayed more often than others, such as American's 1309 from Boston to Chicago, which was late by an average of fifty-four minutes 84 percent of the time. Delta Airlines had 11 flights delayed 70 percent or more of the time; flight 1992 from Atlanta to New York Kennedy was delayed 97 percent of the time by an average of eighty-two minutes.

Will children know what to do when they are delayed? They probably do not know about the FAA's Rule 240, which states that airlines who have delayed flights because of human error should put passengers on the next available flight at no cost. Do not put children on the last flight of the day, because if something goes awry, they may find themselves alone all night in a strange airport. Try to limit the number of transfers a child will have to make; a direct flight or train is always preferable. Find out the name of the escorts or drivers and talk with them before transporting children. Check out the route, since curves, traffic patterns, average speed of travel, and neighborhood configuration might be important considerations; some roads are safer than others. Have someone meet the taxi to ensure that children arrive where they're supposed to be safely. Make sure your children have contingency options in case situations don't work out as planned. The more parents anticipate the unexpected, the better they can prevent problems.

Realize transportation providers aren't babysitters.

The primary responsibility of people hired to transport other people's kids is to get children safely to and from their destinations. Amusing young passengers is not part of the job description. Parents need to realize this and not assume that workers will provide extraordinary attention to their children. Unaccompanied minors are generally treated the same way as adult passengers. There is variability in how children are treated by transportation workers, with some being extremely attentive while others barely acknowledge the presence of the child. The manner in which drivers respond to children depends upon their style, not job their description. For instance, some bus drivers are very nurturing, others are authoritarian, and some are detached. Realize that children may throw things that belong to other students out the window, destroy their homework, poke, jab, pinch, hit, spit, or make riders—especially small, young ones—afraid or uncomfortable. Sometimes students bring weapons, drugs, or other inappropriate items on buses. Most drivers do not have an adult assistant on board to specifically monitor children's behaviors, and they do the best they can. In most ways, children traveling alone are on their own. Children who fare best are those who have been well-prepared by their parents, who understand what is going to happen, what they are supposed to do, where they are supposed to go, and are equipped with backpacks full of snacks and things to amuse them. To reduce the potential risk for children, organizations should carefully screen and train any individual who will be providing transportation and require drivers to have a chauffeur license, which is proof of a higher standard than the "anyone who can drive" approach. Most don't.

Sign releases.

Parents should expect to sign permission forms if their child is to be transported by organizations like schools, churches, Scouts, sports, or recreational groups. The organization should provide parents with these forms ahead of time. This will help protect the organization for insurance purposes. Parents need to know when their children will be in a vehicle, where they are going, with whom they are traveling, and when they will return.

Buckle kids up and consider where they sit.

Child safety seats reduce the risk of death by 70 percent for infants and 55 percent for toddlers, and booster seats decrease injuries for older children. In a study of the use of child safety seats in over 4,000 vehicles, researchers found that child safety seats were only used in half to two-thirds of the time for children under sixty pounds. Only in 20 percent of the cases were the seats properly installed and used. Studies have found that fewer than 10 percent of five to eight-year-olds use booster seats. Before cars had seat belts, kids regularly flew off the seats or out of windows upon impact. Where children sit impacts their safety. The front passenger seat in a car is a dangerous spot for children because of impact and airbag injuries. Young children should never be placed in the front seat of the car. Adults who believe that kids who sit in the back seat do not need to wear seat belts because they are safe there are incorrect, since an unbelted child in the rear is at as much risk as a belted child in front. Volvo found that in a crash at thirty miles per hour, unbelted children in the back can kill or injure passengers in the front seat when they fly forward. Small bodies can crash against the roof, dashboard, and steering wheel or be thrown out of the car, especially if they're not wearing seatbelts. While seatbelts have been proven to prevent injury and death, three out of ten Americans still don't wear them or buckle up their children, according to the National Highway Traffic Safety Administration. Insurance experts recommend that all children twelve and younger should ride buckled-up in the back seat. Children under age thirteen who sat in rear seats were 50 percent less likely to die in a crash than children in the front passenger seat. Riding in the back seat is associated with a 46 percent reduction in the risk of fatal injury in cars with a front passenger–side airbag and at least a 30 percent reduction in the risk of fatal injury in cars with no front passenger–side airbag. Most cars are hit on the driver side rather than the front passenger side, so it is safer for kids not to sit behind the driver. In general, the safest seat for a child is the center rear seat. Yet a recent survey found that a quarter of children under twelve rode in the front seat at least half the time, and that as children became older they were more likely to ride there.

Be wary of substance users and very young, very old, or new drivers.

Driver characteristics must be considered when putting children into vehicles. The age of the driver influences their driving ability. New drivers do not have the skill or experience to anticipate and avoid problems; teenage drivers make up 7 percent of the nation's total licensed drivers, but are involved in 16 percent of all police-reported crashes. Auto accidents are the leading cause of death for teens. Older drivers tend to have slower reaction time and compromised vision and hearing, which may put children at risk when quick reaction time and sharp vision are necessary to avoid accidents. Drivers who have health problems or other limitations may be less able to prevent accidents. Some drivers are on prescription medications that make them drowsy or otherwise compromise their ability to prevent accidents; if they have forgotten to take their medication, normally safe drivers may suddenly become risky ones. And parents must never allow their kids to ride with drivers who may drink and drive. The Centers for Disease Control have found that drinking drivers are responsible for most deaths of children under age fifteen when there are automobile accidents.

PROMISING PROGRAMS

Parents can ensure safer transportation for children. They have been instrumental in demanding manufacturing and training improvements that decrease risk. School buses, automobiles, and planes have all become safer structurally and policy-wise toward the transportation of children as a result. Infants and young children are required to ride in safety seats in most states, because safety seats have been found to save lives. New cars are now routinely installed with airbags, and children are now supposed to ride in the back seat to prevent them from injury. Children are encouraged to wear bicycle helmets and are required to wear helmets when they accompany adults on motorcycles. They are not allowed to drive cars until they are sixteen years old and have undergone driving instruction and passed a test to ensure that they are safe drivers. It has become acceptable social behavior that adults are not supposed to drink and drive, and groups like Mothers Against Drunk Driving have helped pass stricter alcohol laws, which have decreased the numbers of passenger deaths.

There is still a long way to go. Despite mandates from a variety of professional and health organizations, seat belts are not installed on buses, primarily because the cost would run about $2,000 more per bus to cover the cost of $1.80 per belt per child per year. Allan Ross, president of the National Coalition for School Bus Safety, said, "Unfortunately, the school bus industry is a very large and economically powerful industry that grosses about $12 billion annually. With that type of economic power, they are able to have lobbyists in every capitol in the country as well as in Washington, D.C. As a result, the big yellow school bus that is an American icon has basically not changed in over twenty years, which is a sad fact given our technology today." On a $70,000 bus that lasts ten years, the cost is about a penny a day, with added benefits of improved discipline on the school bus. Manufacturers are not likely to install seatbelts without a mandate from Washington, and without widespread pressure from parents, the federal government is unlikely to push for change. Local programs such as Kathy English's SECURE School Bus Safety Program emphasize responsible riders and seek to educate bus drivers, parents, and school personnel about helping kids to be safer. Small, well-intended but isolated programs are no replacement for a system that puts costs over child safety. Better driver and attendant training, child safety seats on planes, seat belts on buses, and assistants on school buses and subways could decrease risk and increase well-being for children. As a simple comparison, many European countries require restraints on their buses to transport children. They do not use school buses, they use motorcoaches, which are safer. Money is a big factor in policy-making decisions that influence child safety. If parents want safer transportation systems and items like seatbelts on planes and buses, they have the power to demand, and receive them—but they do so knowing there will be a price to pay, either way.

American Academy of Pediatrics
141 Northwest Point Blvd.
Elk Grove Village, IL 60007
(847) 434-4000
http://www.aap.org

National Safety Council
1121 Spring Lake Drive
Itasca, IL 60143-3201
(630) 285-1121
http://www.nsc.org

National Association of State Directors
of Pupil Transportation Services
6298 Rock Hill Road
The Plains, VA 20198
(540) 253-5524
http://www.nasdpts.org

Nonprofit Risk Management Center
1130 Seventeenth Street, NW, Suite 210
Washington, DC 20036
(202) 785-3891
http://www.nonprofitriskmanagement
.com

National Coalition for School Bus Safety
PO Box 1616
Torrington, CT 06790-1616
(860) 489-1234
http://www.ncsbs.org

School Bus Fleet
49 S. Maple St.
Marlton, NJ 08053
(856) 596-0999
http://www.schoolbusfleet.com

National Highway Traffic Safety
Administration
400 Seventh Street, SW
Washington, DC 20590
(888) 327-4236
http://www.nhtsa.dot.gov/people/injury

U.S. Department of Transportation
Federal Aviation Administration (FAA)
800 Independence Avenue, SW
Washington, DC 20591
1-866-TELL-FAA (1-866-835-5322)
http://www.faa.gov

REFERENCES

Adams, Marilyn. "Aggravating Delays Still Plague U.S. Travelers." *USA Today*, 16 September 2002. http://www.usatoday.com/travel/news/bonus/2002-09-17-late.htm#more.

———. "Child Safety Up in the Air." *USA Today*, 11 January 2000, 5.

Boston Sunday Globe. "Bans Are Eased on Children Flying Alone." 3 February 2002, M13.

Cable News Network. "Airline Promises Action After Girl Lost On Flight." 17 July 2001. http://www.cnn.om/travel.

———. "Britney Defends Driving With Son on Lap." 2006. http://www.cnn.

com/2006/SHOWBIZ/Music/02/07/
people.britney.spears.ap/index.html.

Caplow, Madlen, and Carol Runyan.
"Parental Responses to a Child Bicycle
Helmet Ordinance," *American Journal
of Preventive Medicine* 11, no. 6
(November 1995): 3371–3374.

Center for Disease Control. "Injuries and
Deaths Among Children Left
Unattended in or Around Motor
Vehicles—United States." July 2000–
June 2001. http://www.cdc.gov/
mmwr/preview/mmwrhtml/mm
5126a3.htm.

———. "National Child Passenger Safety
Week." 2002. http://www.cdc.gov/
ncipc/duip/spotlite/chldseat.htm.

"Childhood Injuries Are No Accident." http:
//www.tf.org/tf/injuries/child4.pdf.

"Consumer Pay Off: Rule 240." 9 May
2001. http://extratv.warnerbros.com/
reframe.html?http://extratv.
warnerbros.com/dailynews/
consumer/05_01/05_09a.html.

Decina, Lawrence, and Kathleen Knoebel.
"Child Safety Seat Misuse Patterns in
Four States." *Accident Analysis and
Prevention* 29, no. 1 (January 1997):
125–132.

DeConto, Jesse. "School Bus Driver Fired."
Portsmouth Herald, 18 April 2002, A1.

Ellement, John. "Woman Is Killed in
Collision With Day Care Van." *Boston
Globe,* 1 May 2002, B1.

Epinions. "Airline Horror Stories." http://
www.epinions.com/trvl-review-
1208–11CC268E-3976FF2A-prod2.

"Guideline For the Safe Transportation of
Pre-School Age Children in School
Buses." http://www.nhtsa.dot.gov/
people/injury/buses/Guidel999/
prekfinal.htm. 1999.

Independent Traveler. "Children Flying
Solo." 2004. http://www.
independenttraveler.com/resources/
article.cfm?AID=203&categor.

Johnson, Glen. "School Buses Found Safer
Than Vans." *Associated Press,* 9 June
1999.

Loring, Pamela. "Seat Belts on School Buses
Becomes Issue For More Than Parents."
The World, 10 February 10 1999.

Los Angeles Times. "Girl Crisscrosses U.S.
in Airline Mix-Up." 18 July 2001, 13.

Mattern, Hal. "Airline Red-faced Over
Girl's Ordeal: 11-Year-Old Suffers 18-
Hour Odyssey." *The Arizona Republic,*
17 July 2001, B1.

Maxa, Rudy. "Avoiding Flight Delays."
Savvy Traveler: Marketplace. http://
www.savvytraveler.org/show/
marketplace/2000/05.30.html.

Morin, Brad. "Police Seize Child Porn at
Cab Driver's Home." *Foster's Daily
Democrat,* 3 October 2001, A1.

National Highway Traffic Safety
Aassociation. "NHTSA Announces
Safety Recalls." *U.S. Department of
Transportation New.* 21 August 1996.

———. "School Bus Safety Belts: Their
Use, Carryover Effects and
Administrative Issues." Washington,
D.C.: National Highway Traffic Safety
Association, 1986.

New Jersey Institute of Technology. "School Bus Safety Belt Study." 1989.

New York Times. "The Safest Seat in a Car." 10 June 2001, 30NE.

Ross, Alan. "National Coalition for School Bus Safety: Torrington, CT." *Associated Press,* 12 April 2001.

Ruben, David. "Transportation Safety." *Parenting Magazine* (September 1998).

Schiavo, Mary. "Flying Blind, Flying Safe." *Time Magazine* (31 March 1997): 52–62.

Schmidt, Peter. "Steer Bus Drivers Away From Violence." *The Education Digest* 61 (January 1996): 8–11.

Spencer, A. "Calling All Consumers." *Consumer's Research Magazine* (12 June 1994).

Transportation Research Board. "National Research Council, Special Report No. 222." 1989.

Wasik, John. "Special Report: Airline Safety." *Consumer's Digest* (July 1997).

Chapter 11 Safety at School

I was in third grade when the principal of our elementary school stormed into our classroom smacking a paddle in his hand, demanding that a classmate, Jimmy, come with him. Jimmy, who did not feel safe going with the enraged principal, figured out that he could not escape from the classroom. He wrapped his arms and legs around his wooden desk and chair as the wild-eyed principal screamed at him to get out of his seat. The principal raced across the room and lunged at the boy, who cowered in his desk for protection. We watched our principal lift the paddle and hit Jimmy dozens of times, shattering the wooden desk and chair as he hit the boy hard wherever he could make contact. We saw him hit the boy on the backside, legs, shoulders, arms, head, and face. All of the children in the class thought our principal had gone crazy, and we hid under our desks, waiting for him to turn his wrath upon us. When Jimmy's desk had finally splintered apart, he dragged the boy, crying and begging for release, into the corner bathroom where we heard the paddle hit the boy, over and over. After what seemed like an eternity, they exited the bathroom, the principal marching the bruised and blistered boy to the office, while the rest of us clung to each other, dreading his return. What caused this violent episode? Only later did we learn that Jimmy's infraction was that he had urinated in the corner of the playground when the teacher refused to let him come inside at recess to relieve himself.

This act of corporal punishment occurred forty years ago in Indiana, where corporal punishment is still allowed. It was long before the tragedy at Columbine High School in Colorado, where students seized control of their school and massacred classmates. How safe are schools today? No child-oriented institution has come under attack regarding child safety as much as schools. While the safety of schools varies from place to place, in general, schools are very safe environments for children. Public schools have actively pursued ways to make themselves safer, and they have succeeded in most communities. Since the school shootings at Columbine, schools have scrutinized themselves, and have certainly been scrutinized by others, to ensure that children will be safe. Visitors aren't allowed unless authorized by the office, metal detectors screen students as they enter each morning and are met by police officers. Anti-bully programs are regular parts of curriculum, and students are encouraged to get along with others. Fire drills are now replaced by terrorist attack practices. Despite these efforts, some parents remain fearful and have pulled students out of public schools and placed them in private or home schools.

The reality is that youth is a high-risk developmental stage of life no matter where kids go to school. Violent injuries and crimes are not rare events for American children. Homicide is the second-leading cause of death for young adults after auto accidents; suicide is the third-leading cause of young people's deaths. But less than 1 percent of all homicides and suicides among school-aged children occur in or around school grounds. Students are much more likely to be victims away from school. The numbers of children hurt at school has dropped to about half of what it had been a decade before.

Schools have seriously addressed their legal duty for care, which includes maintaining safe premises and hiring safe adult role models. The tradition of in loco parentis assumes that schools will watch over children by acting in the role of a parent. This means that they will protect students from willful and wanton misconduct through the enforcement of rules and regulations. But safety standards may vary according to the philosophy and rules of particular schools.

TYPES OF SCHOOLS

Public schools.

There are over forty-six million students enrolled in the nation's public schools from kindergarten through twelfth grade. Public schools are financed from local, state, and federal government sources and must admit all students who live within the borders of their district. The notion of public education was founded by Thomas Jefferson, who felt that equal access to education was the foundation of democracy. Public schools hire professional administrators and teachers who meet state educational requirements. Most are guided by elected school board members and reflect local community values and needs.

Charter schools. A sub-type of public school are charter schools, which are autonomous, alternative public schools, which may receive tax dollars but also have have private funding. Charter schools adhere to the basic curricular requirements of the state but have more flexibility about how to implement regulations and operations.

Magnet schools. Another type of public school is the magnet school, which is a highly competitive, selective public school known for special programs, superior facilities, and high academic standards. Magnet schools may specialize in a particular area, such as the arts or sciences. For instance, Grand Rapids, Michigan, public schools had one located at the city's zoo, where students could specialize in biology and animal studies. Students who apply to magnet schools usually go through a rigorous testing and application process.

Private schools.

Over six million students attend private schools in the United States. These schools rely on tuition payments and funds from nonpublic sources such as religious organizations, endowments, grants, and charitable donations. They may select the students they want from their applicant pool and reject who they don't want on the basis of their own criteria. About 25 percent of the elementary and secondary schools in the United States are private.

Independent schools. Independent schools are private, nonprofit schools governed by elected boards of trustees, and include schools such as Phillips, Andover, and Exeter. Independent schools draw their funds from tuition payments, charitable contributions, and endowments rather than from taxes or church funds. They may be affiliated with a religious institution but cannot receive funds or governance from them. Only 1,500 of the 28,000 private schools are independent, and most are members of the National Association of Independent Schools, which means they have met a standard for accreditation. Many provide students with excellent high school education that is of the caliber provided at some colleges.

Proprietary schools. On the other hand, proprietary schools are private schools that are run for profit. Most do not answer to any board of trustees or elected officials. They are designed to meet market demands, and their philosophy and practices may vary rapidly as a result. Many belong the National Independent Private Schools Association.

Parochial schools. Parochial schools are religiously run schools and constitute the largest number of private schools in the United States. Their academic curriculum is supplemented with required daily religious instruction and prayer. Teachers may be clergy or lay persons, who may or may not be trained educators. Most are poorly paid. Students do not have to personally embrace the overarching religious ideology, but they are required to attend religious education classes and prayer services. Schools run by religious organizations frequently operate under their own mandate, create their own rules, and do not hold their operations accountable to the same educational or disciplinary standards or requirements as publicly funded schools.

Therapeutic schools. Parents who want their troubled children to receive education and therapy at the same facility often seek therapeutic schools. They may be referred to as boarding schools, emotional growth schools, residential treatment schools, or boot camps. There are hundreds of these schools; most tend to be expensive. Some are well-established and housed on large campuses, while others may occur informally, such as in a teacher's home. The Independent Educational Consultants Association lists 250 schools that it considers reputable, but new ones open at the rate of three per month. When parents are frantic about how to help their children, many consider therapeutic schools without understanding that some use techniques that are designed to break the spirit of rebellious youth. Parents should be extremely careful if they choose this type of school, because they vary from being wonderful (such as the Crotched Mountain School in New Hampshire) to being dangerous.

HOW TO CHOOSE A SAFE SCHOOL

Things parents can look for in determining the safety of schools include:

School philosophy and practices.

Each school has its own philosophy, which determines practices and procedures. This is especially the case with private schools. Parents need to identify a school whose ideological principles adhere to their own. Student handbooks, behavior management plans, and the school district's student code of conduct should clearly state the school's position and mirror its philosophy.

Staff qualifications.

In general, people who are well-trained professionals interact more appropriately with children. The qualifications of people who work in schools varies widely. Public school teachers are encouraged to have Master's degrees, and even lower-ranking personnel—such as aides—are expected to have a college degree and experience. Independent schools also tend to hire qualified personnel, although private schools don't have to hire people with teaching degrees or education certification. Schools like Taft and Choate cater to an elite student population and by necessity tend to hire people with good qualifications. Other types of private schools may not use the same level of academic rigor in hiring: parochial schools may place a major importance on the criteria of faith when they hire people, and proprietary schools may value expertise and image in order to capture market-share of students. Parents may send their children to therapeutic schools more for treatment than education. As a general rule, well-trained teachers create safer and more-supportive environments.

Background checks.

Schools that do thorough employee and volunteer background checks are more likely to identify applicants who have problems or a history that would make them a risk around kids. For instance, recent information indicates that some Catholic schools hired teachers who had previously been accused of sexually abusing children. Checks give schools confidence that employees and volunteers will be appropriate and competent and can reassure parents that the school has done everything it can to prevent risk.

Resource availability.

Schools that have access to the intellectual, material, and interpersonal resources that students need create safer institutions. Students who are challenged and provided with creative learning options tend to be more engaged with the task of learning and less invested in problematic behaviors. This does not mean that rich schools are safer than poor ones; it means that students who attend schools where they can get what they need fare better than those who don't. Schools that have guidance departments, school social workers, and ombudsmen are likely to find ways to resolve problems that prevent violence from occurring.

Zero-tolerance policies.

Policies that clearly state that discrimination, violence, and inappropriate behavior will not be allowed—and schools that actively enforce those policies—create more-respectful and less-problematic climates than schools that do not. This includes having policies that limit substance abuse, sexual harassment, gangs, or bullying behavior. No-touch policies help keep kids safe.

School security.

Schools can be made more secure when the main office is by the front door so staff can observe who comes and goes. Visitors should register and wear a name tag so staff can identify whether strangers have received approval from school authorities to be present. Some schools have hired police or resource officers to roam the halls, installed metal detectors, prohibited certain types of clothing, and mandated the use of clear backpacks. Violence prevention programs are also critical to the creation of safe schools. But one of the best ways to ensure a safe school is to create positive experiences for students to learn how to understand, appreciate, and value one another.

Town-gown relationship.

The way schools work with community leaders is an indication of what parents can expect. What happens inside the school is a reflection of what is going on in the community. Schools can't be safe until safety is a priority in the community. Good communication and positive working relationships are signs of support.

School crisis response or safety plan.

Schools that have anticipated potential problems and developed prevention or response plans are probably safer environments for children in the event of an unexpected emergency. Parents are reassured when they know where their children will be and how they will be managed during a crisis.

After-school alternatives.

Schools can be the major organizing factor in a child's life, and if extracurricular activities are available and encouraged, children may avoid problems at home and on the street. The majority of teen violence, substance use, and sexual experimentation tend to occur between the time school is over and when parents come home. Having constructive, monitored academic, recreational, social, and sports programs can all support children and provide a structure that prevents problems.

Corporal punishment.

Historically, part of a teacher's role has been to discipline unruly students. Today hitting a child is considered abuse, and with good reason. More than half of the states ban its use, and some local school boards voluntarily prohibit it in states where corporal punishment is allowed. Yet over 250,000 children are hit yearly in schools with a disproportionate number being minority children and children with disabilities. Corporal punishment is any intervention designed to inflict physical pain in order to motivate a student to stop or change a behavior. In the United States, the most typical form of school corporal punishment is the striking of a student's buttocks with a wooden paddle by a school authority, because the authority believes the student has disobeyed a rule. Many private schools use corporal punishment, especially religious and therapeutic schools; the only state that forbids its use in private schools is New Jersey. If a school has to hit a child to control behavior, this is a red flag of risk.

Punitive education.

Sometimes schools will force students to engage in behaviors they don't define as abusive, but are certainly inappropriate and punitive. Sitting with a dunce hat in the corner or keeling for hours may not be considered abusive, but it is uncomfortable. Staff members at St. Louis's Heartland Christian Academy, whose motto is "Jesus Is the Answer," had criminal charges filed after they allegedly sent eleven misbehaving teenagers to shovel bacteria-filled manure for hours in a pit that was up to their chests.

Diversity.

If schools are the training ground for the world, the reality is that the world is a diverse place, and students are better prepared to be successful when they know how to get along with others. Some schools overtly or covertly allow racial, sexual, homophobic, gender, class, religious, or ethnic tensions to exist. These tensions increase the chances of fear and risk. Other schools actively cultivate environments of sensitivity and support. Exposure to diverse student populations may instill experiences and values that help students to bridge differences. It is common for children to be afraid of people who are different, so providing students the opportunity to find commonalities can overcome risks. Well-trained teachers can help students to overcome biases and make friendships with people who are different from themselves. Diversity can help students to build attitudes and ideas for a smarter and safer tomorrow.

Sexual abuse.

Sexual abuse in U.S. schools is very rare, consisting of only 1 percent of child sexual abuse cases. However, students may be sexually abused by teachers, coaches, or other students. Parents are encouraged to find out how overnight trips will be monitored. Teaching children about good-touch and bad-touch when they are young may empower them to avoid sexually risky situations later in life.

Weapons.

According to a National Adolescent Student Health Survey, as many as 90,000 to 100,000 students carry a gun or weapon to school every day. Usually they do so in communities where gun control is lax. Strong antigun and antiviolence policies in the community will result in a student population that is less likely to feel they need to bring weapons to school.

Bullying.

Bullying is a common occurrence between boys and girls alike. Boys are more likely to engage in physical aggression, while girls are more likely to use emotional and social maltreatment to bully others. Teachers vary widely in their identification and interception of bullying behavior, so parents will want to find out if there is a clear bullying policy in the school with implemented punishments for perpetrators.

Gangs.

Gang behavior is risky for all students, and gangs are being found in rural as well as urban and suburban schools. Gang behavior, when ignored, can grow and become a significant problem, so parents are encouraged to find out if gangs exist and, if so, how the school handles gang members. According to the director of the gang intervention program at the Boston Police Department, young gang members act like normal kids most of the time, and they will respond to respectful direction. Learning more about the gang's motivations and behavior will make it easier for schools to prevent problems. Schools that take a firm antigang position are a safer place for students, and communities that have active gang-prevention programs help keep kids safer.

Truancy and dropout rates.

Successful schools have low absence, tardiness, and dropout rates. Schools where students are unhappy have higher rates. While there can be many reasons for such rates, they are an indicator of student satisfaction, which is related to risk or safety.

Vandalism.

If students show respect for their school and make efforts to care for it, it is a sign of safety; vandalism is a sign of risk, since it illustrates underlying, unresolved conflict.

PROMISING PROGRAMS

A variety of federal, state, and private organizations have united together to help make schools safer, including the Center for Disease Control; National Institute of Mental Health; Departments of Education, Health, and Human Services; National Institute of Justice; and National Institute of Child Health and Human Development, to name but a few. They conclude that financial investment in early-childhood education and prevention programs will yield higher success than any post-problem treatment effort. A study by professor Mark A. Cohen of Vanderbilt University estimates that for each high-risk youth prevented from adopting a life of crime, the country would save $1.7 million. A Rand Corporation report shows that, even without counting the savings to crime victims and society, the resulting savings to government alone from effective early-childhood programs exceeds the cost of the programs by two to four times. Child safety and good education go hand in hand. Investing in early-childhood education pays off in the long run. Good education for children begins with having teachers who are well trained. Resources must be provided to both students and teachers throughout the year so that both can develop their skills. Problems, both educational and social, can be prevented when communities invest in their children.

RESOURCES

Center for the Prevention of School Violence
1801 Mail Service Center
Raleigh, NC 27699-1801
(800) 299-6054
http://www.cpsv.org

Embrace Diversity in Schools
7807 Bluecurl Circle
Springfield, VA 22152
(703) 644-3039
http://www.embracediverseschools.com

Fight Crime
School Violence
http://www.fightcrime.org/reports/
schoolviol.htm

Gang Resistance Education and Training
Program (GREAT)
(800) 726-7070
http://www.great-online.org

Healthy Schools
PO Box 8817
Silver Springs, MD 20907
(800) CDC-INFO
http://www.cdc.gov/HealthyYouth/
index.htm

Keep Schools Safe
http://www.keepschoolssafe.org

National Association of Independent
Schools
1620 L Street, NW, Suite 1100
Washington DC, 20036–5695
(202) 973-9700
http://www.nais.org

National Association of School
Psychologists
4340 East West Highway, Suite 402
Bethesda, MD 20814
(301) 657-0270
http://www.nasponline.org/inform
ation/pospaper_corppunish.html

National Center for the Study of Corporal
Punishment and Alternatives
Temple University
253 Ritter South
Philadelphia, PA 19122
(215) 204-6091
http://www.temple.edu/education/pse/
NCSCPA.html

National Center for Education Statistics
1990 K Street, NW
Washington, DC 20006
(202) 502-7300
http://nces.ed.gov

National Coalition to Abolish Corporal
Punishment in Schools
155 W. Main St., Suite 1603
Columbus, OH 43215
(614) 221-8829
http://www.stophitting.com/
disatschool/facts.php

National PTA
541 N. Fairbanks Court
Suite 1300
Chicago, IL 60611-3396
(312) 670-6782 or (800) 307-4782
http://www.pta.org

National Resource Center for Safe
Schools
Northwest Regional Educational
Laboratory
101 S.W. Main Street, Suite 500
Portland, OR 97204
http://www.nwrel.org

National Safe Kids Campaign
Safe Kids Worldwide
1301 Pennsylvania Ave., NW
Suite 1000
Washington, DC 20004-1707
(202) 662-0600
http://www.safekids.org/tier2_rl.cfm?
folder_id=181

National School Safety Center
141 Duesenberg Drive, Suite 11
Westlake Village, CA 91362
(805) 373-9977
http://www.nssc1.org

Private School Association
1800 Pembrook Drive, Suite 300
Orlando, FL 32810
(407) 522-0124
http://www.npsag.com

United States Center for Disease Control
1600 Clifton Rd.
Atlanta, GA 30333
(800) 311-3435 or (404) 699-3311
http://www.cdc.gov

United States Department of Education
400 Maryland Ave., SW
Washington, DC 20202
(800) 872-5327
http://www.ed.gov/index.jhtml

REFERENCES

American Bar Association. "Gun Violence in Schools." 2005. http://www.abanet.org/gunviol/schoolshm.html.

Angier, Natalie. "Bully for You: Why Push Comes to Shove." *New York Times,* 20 May 2001, 4.1.

Boland, Maureen. "School Types." Parent Center. http://parentcenter.babycenter.com/refcap/bigkid/gpreschool/67288.html.

Braveman, Stephen L. "Sexual Abuse of Children." 2005. www.redshift.com/~braveman.

Carnegie Council on Adolescent Development. "A Matter of Time: Risk and Opportunity in the Out-of-School Hours." Carnegie Corporation of New York, July 1994.

Chmelyns, Carol. "Is Paddling On Its Way Back?" *School Board News.* Alexandria, Va.: National School Boards Association. 5 December 1995. http://www.corpun.com/ussc9512.htm.

David, Phillips. "Threats of Corporal Punishment as Verbal Aggression." *Child Abuse and Neglect* 20, no. 4 (1996): 289–304.

DeVoe, Jill. "Indicators of School Crime and Safety 2002." National Center for Education Statistics and Bureau of Justice Statistics. 2002. http://nces.ed.gov/pubs2003/2003009.pdf.

Elbedour, Salman, Bruce Center, Geoffrey Maruyama, and Avi Assor. "Physical and Psychological Maltreatment in Schools." *School Psychology International* 18, no. 3 (1997): 201–215.

Foster's Daily Democrat. "Newton

Principal Resigns Over Drug Case."
Foster's Daily Democrat, 4 November
1999, A16.

———. "Teacher Faces Child Sex
Charges." *Foster's Daily Democrat,* 2
October 1999, A14.

Letter, Kim. "Ex-janitor Sentenced for
Attempted Sexual Assault." *Foster's
Daily Democrat,* 10 November 1999, A3.

National Organizations Seeking
Abolition of Corporal Punishment in
Schools. "Exposing 'Dirty Secrets'
Legislation Will Make It Easier to
Identify Abusive Teachers." 7 May
2000. http://www.temple.edu/
education/pse/NCSCPA.html.

Rakowsky, Judy. "Principal Was
Unconvinced of Charges." *Boston
Globe,* 3 November 1999, B3.

Sanders, Bob. "Teen After School
Programs Fall Short." *Foster's Sunday
Citizen,* 17 October 1999, A13.

Sherman, Lawrence, et al. "Preventing
Crime." 2005. http://www.ncjrs.org/
works/index.htm.

Umansky, Diane. "The Middle School
Squeeze." *Working Mothers* (February
1999): 27–34.

United States Department of Education.
"Annual Report of School Safety."
1998. http://www.ed.gov/pubs/
AnnSchoolRept98/index.html.

"Teacher's Pet? Girls Face Sexual Abuse in
Schools." *Secretariat* ID21 (October
2001).

Zill, Nicholas, and Mary Collins. *National
Household Education Survey:
Approaching Kindergarten: A Look at
Preschoolers in the United States.*
Washington, D.C.: National Center for
Education Statistics, 1995.

Chapter 12 Conclusion

This book has addressed the phenomenon of risk anxiety as it pertains to the issue of child safety. Parents have wanted to believe that other people take good care of our kids because we *need* to believe that. We have relied on trust when there is no basis for it. We have used denial and ignorance to reduce our worry. We have assumed that there is a system in place to protect children when none actually exists. There is always a risk when children are cared for by other people; the question must be: is it an acceptable risk?

Parents could make children safer by finding out more about the people who oversee our children's care and by knowing more about the kind of care that children receive. That information is usually readily available if parents simply take the time to look. Parents must also learn how to better communicate with their children; they should better learn how to listen and how to encourage their children to feel safe enough to talk with them about difficult topics. It requires active parental involvement, from identifying the best care situation to monitoring the care situation across time. Because there is no national system to ensure safety, parents have no choice except to decide for themselves if care situations and providers are safe.

The information presented throughout this book confirms a set of conclusions that points out how:

- Most children are safe when they are in the care of other people. But not all providers are competent or safe. Even among those who are, necessary safeguards may not have been put into place, and a moment of forgetfulness or negligence can create needless injury or tragedy.
- Blind trust is not enough when it comes to leaving your precious children in the care of other people. Parents need to have reason why they can trust others to take good care of their children.
- Maltreatment, neglect, abuses, and risk are more common than parents would like to think.
- While no situation is ever risk-free, it is possible to reduce the number of factors that put children at risk if parents are active participants in the

caregiving process, from the initial background screening to ongoing monitoring of care.

- Partnership arrangements between parents and providers are essential for good child care. It helps if there are pre-established guidelines for how they will partner together, especially as it pertains to dealing with expectations, communication, or conflict.
- While caregivers may truly love the child, the act of caregiving is also a moral, legal, and business relationship.
- Delegated care provided by other people has not been a national priority.
- Few standards for delegated caregiving exist, and those which do are seldom enforced.
- Continuous monitoring and periodic evaluations of care providers seldom occur by anyone other than the parent.
- There is a greater chance of external monitoring occurring when caregivers are part of a larger organization where there are more people to observe behaviors and intervene when problems emerge.

Reasons why children are needlessly at risk when in the care of other people could be easily addressed. Caregivers who are poorly trained, overworked, underpaid, and inadequately supervised pose risks for kids. Caregivers who are well-trained, well-paid, well-monitored, and treated like valued professionals do a better job caring for other people's kids. Those who have professional credentials, expertise, and training about how to work successfully with children and youth are much safer bets than those who work with kids because it is convenient. Use of background checks, ongoing monitoring, regular evaluation, and immediate action when incidents occur will help reduce the chances that kids will be hurt. There is no sure-fire guarantee that kids will be safe, but the likelihood is increased when there are clear guidelines and criminal penalties when children are assaulted or abused. Most of the time—as in the case of the home daycare provider in Reading, Massachusetts, who had two babies die while in her care—red risk flags are clearly waving. The provider was unlicensed, she had too many children, there were previous allegations of abuse, and she was poorly trained. In order to avoid such tragedies, parents are advised to look at clear-cut things that can be done now to ensure that all children will be safer.

Laws can help define appropriate care standards for parents and providers. Oversight and credentialing organizations promote better care of children.

When oversight organizations exist, a system of policies, procedures, guidelines, training, monitoring, supervising, and evaluating providers can reduce child abuse. Parents have assumed that someone else has screened the credentials of the people who are watching our children—but in reality, the only "someone" may be the parent. The first line of defense is active, involved parents who are willing to advocate for their children. They have an obligation to partner with providers to ensure that everyone gets their needs met. Caregivers who are respected and well-treated generally tend to be more professional and provide better care to kids

When caregivers are people with whom the parents have an emotional attachment, communication about children's care becomes challenging, particularly when there is conflict or concern. Love and friendship are not necessarily the best criteria to use when selecting someone to provide high-quality care for children. It takes time, effort, and commitment to make sure that children are safe. Organizations like the U.S. Army's daycare program, the public school system, and the American Camping Association have found out that ensuring safety is hard work, and they have designed programs and created standards in order to prevent problems.

All children are "other people's kids." There are times in which all adults are caregivers to others. When parents protect their own children, their actions influence others. When organizations make decisions about how to operate, their youngest consumers are inevitably affected. As parents and providers partner together, the quality of care improves for all children. When all children are safe, healthy, and happy, the world will reflect that outcome.

RESOURCES

Advocates for Youth
2000 M Street, NW, Suite 750
Washington, DC 20036
(202) 419-3420
http://www.advocatesforyouth.org

Carnegie Foundation
Mobilize Communities to Support
Young Children and Their Families
51 Vista Lane
Stanford, CA 94305
(650) 566-5100
http://www.carnegie.org/starting
_points/startp5.html

Center for the Future of Children
Packard Foundation
300 Second St.
Los Altos, CA 94022
(650) 948-7658
http://www.futureofchildren.org

Children Now
1212 Broadway, 5th Floor
Oakland, CA 94612
(510) 763-1974
http://www.childrennow.org

Children's Defense Fund
25 E St., NW
Washington, DC 20001
(202) 628-8787
http://www.childrensdefense.org

Children's Partnership
1351 3rd St. Promenade, Suite 206
Santa Monica, CA 90401
(310) 260-1220
http://www.childrenspartnership.org

Children's Rights Information Network
c/o Save the Children
1 St. John's Lane
London EC1M 4AR
United Kingdom
+44 20 7012 6865
http://www.crin.org

Child Welfare League of America
440 First St., NW, 3rd Floor
Washington, DC 20001
(202) 638-2952
http://www.cwla.org

Committee for Economic Development
2000 L St., NW, Suite 700
Washington, DC 20036
(202) 296-5860
http://www.ced.org

International Bureau for Children's Rights
485 Saint-Mathieu St.
Montreal, Quebec
H341 2P7
Canada
(514) 932-7056
http://www.ibcr.org

Justice for Children
2600 Southwest Freeway, Suite 806
Houston, TX 77098
(713) 225-4357
http://www.jfcadvocacy.org

KidsPeace
The National Center for Kids Overcoming Crisis
5300 KidsPeace Drive
Orefield, PA 18069
(800) 25-PEACE or 1-800-334-4KID
http://www.kidspeace.org

National Association of Child Advocates
Voices for America's Children
1000 Vermont Ave., NW, 7th Floor
Washington, DC 20005
(202) 289-0777
http://www.childadvocacy.org

National Association to Protect Children
46 Haywood Street, Suite 315
Asheville, NC 28801
(828) 350-9350
http://www.protect.org

National Center for Children in Poverty
215 W. 125th Street, 3rd Floor
New York, NY 10027
(646) 284–9600
http://www.nccp.org

National Child Protective Workers
Association
27 Ford Street
Baldwinsville, NY 13027–2328
(315) 635-4791
http://www.childprotective.org

National Children's Alliance
1612 K Street, NW, Suite 500
Washington, DC 20006
(202) 452-6001 or 1-800-239-9950
http://www.nca-online.org

The UN Convention on the Rights of the
Child
333 E. 38th St.
New York, NY 10016
(800) 4-UNICEF
http://www.unicef.org/crc

Voices for America's Children
1522 K Street, NW, #600
Washington DC 20005
(202) 289-0777
http://www.childadvocacy.org

REFERENCES

Amidei, Nancy. "Child Advocacy: Let's Get the Job Done." *Dissent* 40 (1993): 213–220.

Berman, Marshall. "Children of the Future." *Dissent* 40 (1993): 221–225.

Bernier. Jetta "A Battle Plan to Shield the Young From Sex Abuse." *Boston Globe*, 2 June 2002, E1.

Besharov, Douglas. "Toward Better Research on Child Abuse and Neglect: Making Definitional Issues an Explicit Methodological Concern." *Child Abuse and Neglect* 5 (1981): 383–390.

Broder, David. "Now to Rescue Our Children." *Washington Post*, 11–17 March 1991.

Cahill, Brian. "Training Volunteers as Child Advocates." *Child Welfare* (November–December 1986): 545–553.

Caley, Linda M. "Child Advocacy at the Local Level: New Initiatives for Children and their Effect on Public Policy" Ph.D. Disssertation. Buffalo, N.Y.: State University of New York at Buffalo, 1986.

Conger, Janet. "Hostages to Fortune: Youth, Values and the Public Interest. *American Psychologist* (April 1988): 291–301.

Danziger, Sandra, and Sheldon Danziger. "Child Poverty and Public Policy: Toward a Comprehensive Public Policy Agenda." *Daedalus* 122 (1993): 57–84.

De Vita, Carol, and Rachel Mosher-Williams, eds. *Who Speaks for America's Children?* Washington, D.C.: Urban Institute Press, 2001.

Dicker, Sheryl. *Stepping Stones: Successful Advocacy for Children.* New York: Foundation for Child Development, 1990.

Dubowitz, Howard, Maureen Black, Raymond Starr, and Susan Zuravin. "A Conceptual Definition of Child Neglect. Criminal Justice and Behavior." 20, no. 1 (1993): 8–26.

Erwin, Elizabeth J. *Putting Children First: Visions for a Brighter Future for Young Children and Their Families.* Baltimore: Paul H. Brookes, 1996.

Fernandez, Happy Craven. *The Child Advocacy Handbook.* New York: Pilgrim Press, 1980.

Goldstein, Joseph, et.al. *Beyond the Best Interests of the Child.* New York: Free Press, 1973.

Gormley, William T. *Everybody's Children: Child Care as a Problem.* Washington, D.C.: Brookings Institution, 1995.

Graff, Harvey. *Conflicting Paths: Growing Up in America.* Cambridge, Mass.: Harvard University, 1995.

Hagedorn, John M. *Forsaking Our Children: Bureaucracy and Reform in the Child Welfare System.* Chicago: Lake View Press, 1995.

Hamburg, David. *Today's Children: Creating a Future for a Generation in Crisis.* New York: Times Books, 1992.

Hawes, Joseph. *The Children's Rights Movement: A History of Advocacy and Protection.* Boston: Twayne Publishers, 1991.

Hayes, Cheryl D. *Making Policies for Children: A Study of the Federal Process.* Washington, D.C.: National Academy Press, 1990.

Hayes, Cheryl D., et al. *Who Cares for America's Children? Child Care Policy for the 1990s.* Washington, D.C.: National Academy Press, 1990.

Helfer, Ray. "Child Abuse and Neglect: Assessment, Treatment and Prevention." *Child Abuse and Neglect* 11, no. 1 (1991): 3–15.

Hernandez, Donald J. *America's Children: Resources From Family, Government, and the Economy.* New York: Russell Sage Foundation, 1993.

Hewlett, Sylvia. *When the Bough Breaks: The Cost of Neglecting Our Children.* New York: Harper Perennial, 1992.

Kamerman, Sheila B. *Starting Right: How America Neglects Its Youngest Children and What We Can Do About It.* New York: Oxford University Press, 1995.

Knitzer, Jane. "Child Advocacy: A Perspective." *American Journal of Orthopsychiatry* 46, no. 2 (1976): 200–216.

———. "Children's Rights in the Family and Society." *American Journal of Orthopsychiatry* 52, no. 3 (1982): 481–495.

Melton, Gary, and Mary Fran Flood. "Research Policy and Child Maltreatment: Developing the Scientific Foundation for Effective Protection of Children. *Child Abuse and Neglect* 18, no. 1 (1994): 1–28.

Miller, George. *Giving Children a Chance: The Case for More Effective National Policies*. Washington, D.C.: Center for National Policy Press, 1989.

Minow, Martha, and Richard Weissbourd. "Social Movements for Children." *Daedalus* 122 (1993): 1–29.

Mnookin, Robert. *Dividing the Child: Social and Legal Dilemmas*. Boston: Harvard University Press, 1992.

Mnookin, Robert H. *In the Interest of Children: Advocacy, Law Reform, and Public Policy*. New York: W. H. Freeman and Company, 1987.

Moore, Stanley W. *The Child's Political World: A Longitudinal Perspective*. New York: Praeger, 1985.

Prochner, Larry. "Quality of Care in Historical Perspective." *Early Childhood Research Quarterly* 11 (1996): 5–17.

Roberts, Diana. "Child Protection in the 21st Century." *Child Abuse and Neglect* 15, no. 1 (1991): 25–30.

Russakoff, Dale. "In Suburbs, Child Care Is King: Ignored by Politicans, Families Struggle With Costs." *Boston Globe,* 9 July 2002, F8.

Summerfield, Derek. "If Children's Lives Are Precious, Which Children?" *Lancet* 9120 (27 June 1998): 8–9.

Takanishi, Ruby. "Childhood as a Social Issue: Historical Roots of Contemporary Child Advocacy Movements." *Journal of Social Issues* 34 (1978): 8–28.

Thompson, Penny, and Nancy Molyneaux. "Enforcing Child Care Standards: Nobody Is Talking About Enforcement—Without It, Standards Are Meaningless." *Public Welfare* 50 (Winter 1992): 20–25.

Tiffin, Susan. *In Whose Best Interest? Child Welfare Reform in the Progressive Era*. Westport, Conn.: Greenwood Press, 1982.

Tompkins, James R., Benjamin L. Brooks, and Timothy J. Tompkins. *Child Advocacy: History, Theory and Practice*. Durham, N.C.: Carolina Academic Press, 1998.

Welch, Charles. "We Can Do Better For Abused Children." *Boston Globe,* 15 February 2004, A17.

Westman, Jack. *Child Advocacy: New Professional Roles for Helping Families*. New York: Free Press, 1979.

———. "The Child Advocacy Team in Child Abuse and Neglect." *Child Psychiatry and Human Development* (1996): 221–234.

———. "Juvenile Ageism: Unrecognized Prejudice and Discrimination Against the Young." *Child Psychiatry and Human Development* 21, no. 4 (1991): 237–251.

Wilgoren, Jodi. "Quality Day Care, Early,

Is Tied to Achievements as Adult." *New York Times*, 22 October 1999, A16.

Winik, Lyric Wallwork. "Every Child Deserves the Best." *Parade Magazine* (24 January 1999): 4–8.

Wise, Paul H. "Child Rights and the Devaluation of Women." *Health and Human Rights* (1995): 472–476.

Wissow, Lawrence. *Child Advocacy for the Clinician: An Approach to Child Abuse and Neglect*. Baltimore: Williams and Wilkins, 1990.

Appendix A Caregiver Pledge of Commitment to Provide Quality Care to Children

We, as caregivers, have been given the unique and privileged responsibility of caring for other people's children. Precious lives have been entrusted to us so that we may provide caring concern. This means that in every action we must demonstrate the qualities that are essential for helping children grow strong in mind, body, and spirit. Therefore, I pledge to:

Educate myself about children's needs and abilities. It is not enough to care about children; in order to be an effective provider of care, I need to learn about the physical, cognitive, emotional, and social needs of children. Infants, elementary-age children, and teens all have unique needs, so I will seek to educate myself so that I can provide them the best care possible.

Keep children safe from harm. Young bodies and minds are developing and must be subject to special treatment. I will not inflict pain on a child, nor will I allow others to do so. I will not grab, smack, hit, bite, bind, or otherwise hurt a child, nor will I allow anyone else to do so. Sexual exploitation or physical abuse of a child under my care will not be tolerated.

Avoid verbal and emotional abuse of children. I will be careful with the words I use and conversations I have around children, since words can hurt a child as much as physical abuse. There is no need for the children to be exposed to cursing or mean, threatening, or exploitative language. Children should be shielded from certain topics of adult conversation. They do not need to hear about the personal problems or relationships of adults. The words I use will show respect for myself and others. I will avoid uncaring criticism, hateful words, and destructive behavior of all kinds.

Provide clear information about what parents and children should expect. In my caregiving role, I will make clear what I will be doing with the child and what I will not. Likewise, I will expect that parents will complete an application packet of materials so that I know important information about the children and their family, which will enable me to take better care of them. I will try to communicate regularly with the parents and children, listen to their concerns, address potential problem areas, and use my partnership with them to improve the quality of my care. To avoid confusion, critical information will be provided in both written and oral forms.

Use appropriate discipline. Children need to know that I am fair and can be trusted. As a responsible adult, I will sometimes need to redirect children's behavior along a more constructive path. I will do so with discipline, in which I show kindness and educate the child about why other behaviors are better. I will focus on instructive discipline, not punishment, since punishment includes the use of anger, retaliation, and vengeance. If I cannot correct a child's behavior in a positive fashion, I will develop an alternative problem-solving strategy in consultation with experts and parents.

Avoid risky situations. While children are in my care, I will develop knowingly safe activities. I will avoid putting children into situations where they may be hurt or scared. If a situation should unexpectedly become high risk, well-designed alternative and emergency procedures will be implemented.

Guarantee that facilities are safe. The building and other facilities where children will be under my care must meet state safety and public health standards. There must be fire escapes, safe stairways, no exposures to hazardous materials or toxins, etc. Not only will the buildings be safe, but also the grounds, parking lot, equipment, and other associated materials that the child may come in contact with.

Assure that other people are safe and appropriate with children. Whether I hire staff members, use volunteers, or have friends or family members present, my first responsibility is to the safety of the child. It is my obligation to adequately screen staff and volunteers, to provide ongoing monitoring and evaluation of them, and to terminate them if I have questions about their appropriateness with children. If other people drop by and have contact with the children, their visits will be authorized, brief, and not impinge upon my taking good care of them.

Consider the child's developmental and emotional needs. Whether designing a learning activity, a social situation, or a sporting or recreational event, deciding on a disciplinary tactic, or employing the child to do a job, I will take into consideration the child's developmental and emotional needs. I will try to the best of my ability to make sure my decisions are age and child appropriate. I will not tolerate the neglect of any child's needs.

Treat each child as an individual. Every child has unique abilities, gifts, vulnerabilities, and needs. I shall try to be attentive to them and enhance their gifts and help them overcome their weaknesses.

Acknowledge faults. Despite my best attempts, I may not always be able to assure 100 percent safety of the children for whom I am caring. When failures occur, it is my obligation to rectify the situation as best as possible. This may mean changing operating procedures, terminating employees, and notifying the child and his or her parents of the problem and how I intend to address it. If I am not able to ensure the safety of children, I will consider whether it would be better for me to limit my caregiver contact with them.

Accept that I am a role model for children. My behaviors, words, and actions—for good or for ill—influence the children who are around me. I pledge to work to the best of my ability to shelter them from my personal problems, to promote positive and healthy behaviors, to keep them safe from exposure to negative and unhealthy influences, and to promote through my own behavior high values to which they can aspire.

Signed _____

Date _____

Parts of this pledge have been adapted from Dr. Louis Malaguzzi's "A Bill of Three Rights" for the Reggio Emilia program.

Appendix B Parent's Pledge to Promote Safety of Their Children

We, as parents, have been given the most important job on earth—the gift of overseeing the lives of our children. In accepting this responsibility from the moment of their birth forward, we will seek to make sure that their physical, emotional, cognitive, and social foundations will be strong so they may thrive as they grow into adulthood. Knowing that we cannot—and should not—be with them every moment of their lives, we seek to establish positive opportunities for our children to develop healthy and productive relationships with other people. In doing so, we will enable them to make positive contributions to the world in which they live when they are adults and to create an environment that will enable their children's children to create a safe and harmonious world. Therefore, I pledge to:

Conduct a good investigation. I will strive to locate the best person, group, or organization to care for my child. Many people and groups provide care, some are good and some aren't. It is my responsibility to identify the best providers available and see if they will work with my child.

Seek recommendations. I will ask for, and contact, people who can give references about the quality of care my child may expect to receive from a provider. I will also try to determine from friends, organizations, associations, or other people who may know whether the provider is good.

Observe the caregiver in action on multiple occasions. What caregivers actually do is far more important than what they say they are going to do. I will observe the adult providing care at different times of days, in different situations, and when I am not expected in order to gain a clearer sense of the quality of care.

Assume responsibility for making sure organizations or professions that I ask to care for my child have met appropriate licensure, accreditation, credentialing, or other professional standards. It is up to me to make sure that the information that the providers tell me is accurate and up-to-date.

Conduct regular reviews of the care my child receives. I will meet with the provider at appropriate intervals to make sure the care of my child is appropriate.

Confront the provider when I have concerns or suspicions about improprieties. If my child, through behavior or words, indicates that something isn't right when he or she is with the provider, it is my obligation to find out what's really going on. This means talking with other key informants who may have knowledge of the situation, as well as with the provider. Even if it is an emotionally difficult confrontation, it is my job as a parent to make sure my kids are safe.

Listen to my intuition. If something doesn't feel right, it probably isn't.

People must earn my trust. I will not automatically assume that anyone will take good care of my child. Trust should be earned, not assumed.

Report the maltreatment or abuse of my child—or the abuse I have observed of any child—to the proper authorities. When my child is harmed, or if I have witnessed another person's child being harmed, it is my obligation to contact the proper child protection authorities and report it. The child protection authorities will then have the obligation to conduct an investigation to determine if my experience is unique or part of a larger pattern of abuse. If everyone would assume this responsibility, all children would be safer, and no child would have to experience undue abuse or maltreatment.

Keep children's bodies safe from harm. Young bodies are developing and are subject to special treatment. I will not use any part of my body to inflict pain on a child, nor will I allow others to do so. I will not grab, smack, hit, bite, bind, or otherwise hurt a child, nor will I allow anyone else to do so. If a child indicates they have been sexually or physically abused, I must trust them, comfort them, and then determine what happened and seek appropriate action.

Avoid verbal and emotional abuse of children. I will be careful with the words I use and conversations I have around my children as well as around other people's children, because words can hurt a child as much as physical abuse. There is no need for the children to be exposed to cursing, mean, threatening, or exploitative language. Children should be shielded from certain topics of adult conversation. They do not need to hear about my problems. The words I use will show respect for myself and others. I will avoid uncaring criticism, hateful words, and destructive behavior of all kinds.

Provide clear information about what my child's providers should expect. I will give my providers adequate notice if my child's schedule changes, if there are changes in the household, or if my child is experiencing unusually positive or negative events or emotions. In this way, the providers can better meet my child's needs.

Clarify what I consider appropriate discipline. Parents and providers may have different ideas about what is considered appropriate discipline. I will be clear with the provider about how I expect my child to be disciplined.

Avoid placing my child in risky situations. If my child is asked to participate in activities that I believe contain an unusually high degree of risk, it is my obligation to talk with the adult who will be supervising that activity to ensure that the children will be safe. If safety cannot be guaranteed, it is my obligation to deny my child access to activities they want to do or people they may want to see out of concern about his or her well-being.

Check to see that facilities are safe. I will provide reasonable scrutiny to make sure the buildings and other facilities where children will be meet state safety and public health standards.

Determine if other people are safe and appropriate with children. It is my responsibility to ask for information about provider qualifications, experience, training, and credentials. It is also my responsibility to identify if unauthorized people will have access to my child, and if so, what to do about it.

Consider the child's developmental and emotional needs. Every child is different and has his or her own unique set of skills and needs. I will try to find providers who help the children to grow and mature in their strengths and to help them overcome their weaknesses.

Signed _____

Date _____

Parts of this pledge have been adapted from Dr. Louis Malaguzzi's "A Bill of Three Rights" for the Reggio Emilia program.

Appendix C Code of Conduct for Interscholastic Coaches

We believe that youth athletic competition should be fun but that it must also be a significant part of a sound educational program. We believe that those who coach student-athletes are, first and foremost, teachers who have a duty to assure that their sports programs promote important life skills and the development of good character. We believe that the essential elements of character-building are embodied in the concept of sportsmanship and six core ethical values: trustworthiness, respect, responsibility, fairness, caring, and good citizenship (the "Six Pillars of Character"). We further believe that the highest potential of sports is achieved when teacher-coaches consciously Teach, Enforce, Advocate, and Model (T.E.A.M.) these values and are committed to the ideal of pursuing victory with honor. Finally, we believe that sincere and good-faith efforts to honor the words and spirit of this Code will improve the quality of our programs and the well being of our student-athletes. This Code of Conduct applies to all full-time and part-time coaches involved in interscholastic sports. I understand that in my position as a coach, I must act in accord with the following code:

TRUSTWORTHINESS

1. Trustworthiness: be worthy of trust in all I do and teach student-athletes the importance of integrity, honesty, reliability, and loyalty.
2. Integrity: model high ideals of ethics and sportsmanship and always pursue victory with honor; teach, advocate, and model the importance of honor and good character by doing the right thing even when it's unpopular or personally costly.
3. Honesty: don't lie, cheat, steal, or engage in or permit dishonest or unsportsmanlike conduct.
4. Reliability: be on time; fulfill commitments; I will do what I say I will do.
5. Loyalty: be loyal to my school and team; put the team above personal glory.
6. Primacy of Educational Goals: be faithful to the educational and character-development missions of the school and assure that these objectives are not compromised to achieve sports performance goals;

always place the academic, emotional, physical, and moral well-being of athletes above desires and pressures to win.

7. Counseling: be candid with student-athletes and their parents about the likelihood of getting an athletic scholarship or playing on a professional level. Counsel them about the requirement of many colleges preventing recruitment of student-athletes that do not have a serious commitment to their education, the ability to succeed academically or the character to represent their institution honorably.

RESPECT

8. Respect: treat all people with respect all the time and require the same of student-athletes.
9. Class: be a good sport, teach and model class, be gracious in victory, and accept defeat with dignity; encourage student-athletes to give fallen opponents a hand, compliment extraordinary performance, and show sincere respect in pre- and post-game rituals.
10. Taunting: refrain from engaging in or allowing trash talking, taunting, boastful celebrations, or other actions that demean individuals or the sport.
11. Respect Officials: treat contest officials with respect; don't complain about or argue with official calls or decisions during or after an athletic event.
12. Respect Parents: treat the parents of student-athletes with respect; be clear about my expectations, goals, and policies; maintain open lines of communication and expect that parents will respect players and coaches in return.
13. Profanity: refrain from engaging in or permiting profanity or obscene gestures during practices, sporting events, on team buses, or in any other situation where the behavior could reflect badly on the school or the sports program.
14. Positive Coaching: use positive coaching methods to make the experience enjoyable, increase self-esteem, and foster a love and appreciation for the sport; refrain from physical or psychological intimidation, verbal abuse, and conduct that is demeaning to student-athletes or others.
15. Effort and Teamwork: encourage student-athletes to pursue victory with honor, to think and play as a team, to do their best and continually

improve through personal effort and discipline; discourage selfishness and put less emphasis on the final outcome of the contest than upon effort, improvement, teamwork, and winning with character.

16. Professional Relationships: maintain appropriate, professional relationships with student athletes and respect proper teacher-student boundaries. Sexual or romantic contact with students is strictly forbidden, as is verbal or physical conduct of a sexual nature directed to or in view of student-athletes.

RESPONSIBILITY

17. Life Skills: always strive to enhance the physical, mental, social, and moral development of student-athletes and teach them positive life skills that will help them become well-rounded, successful, and socially responsible.

18. Advocate Education: advocate the importance of education beyond basic athletic eligibility standards and work with faculty and parents to help student-athletes set and achieve the highest academic goals possible for them.

19. Advocate Honor: prominently discuss the importance of character, ethics, and sportsmanship in materials about the athletic program and vigorously advocate the concept of pursuing victory with honor in all communications.

20. Good Character: foster the development of good character by teaching, enforcing, advocating, and modeling (T.E.A.M.) high standards of ethics and sportsmanship and the Six Pillars of Character.

21. Role-Modeling: be a worthy role model, always be mindful of the high visibility and great influence I have as a teacher-coach, and consistently conduct myself in private and coaching situations in a manner that exemplifies all I want my student-athletes to be.

22. Personal Conduct: refrain from profanity, disrespectful conduct, and the use of alcohol or tobacco in front of student-athletes or in other situations where my conduct could undermine my positive impact as a role model.

23. Competence: strive to improve coaching competence and acquire increasing proficiency in coaching principles and current strategies, character-building techniques, first aid, and safety.

24. Knowledge of Rules: maintain a thorough knowledge of current game and competition rules and ensure that my student-athletes know and understand the rules.

25. Positive Environment: strive to provide challenging, safe, enjoyable, and successful experiences for the athletes by maintaining a sports environment that is physically and emotionally safe.
26. Safety and Health: be informed about basic first aid principles and the physical capacities and limitations of the age group coached.
27. Unhealthy Substances: educate student-athletes about the dangers and prohibit the use of unhealthy and illegal substances including alcohol, tobacco, and recreational or performance-enhancing drugs.
28. Eating Disorders: counsel students about the dangers of and be vigilant for signs of eating disorders or unhealthy techniques to gain, lose, or maintain weight.
29. Physician's Advice: seek and follow the advice of a physician when determining whether an injured student-athlete is ready to play.
30. Privilege to Compete: ensure that student-athletes understand that participation in interscholastic sports programs is a privilege, not a right, and that they are expected to represent their school, team, and teammates with honor, on and off the field; require student-athletes to consistently exhibit good character and conduct themselves as positive role models.
31. Self-Control: control my ego and emotions; avoid displays of anger and frustration; don't retaliate.
32. Integrity of the Game: protect the integrity of the game; don't gamble; play the game according to the rules.
33. Enforcing Rule: enforce this Code of Conduct consistently in all sports-related activities and venues even when the consequences are high.
34. Protect Athletes: put the well-being of student-athletes above other considerations and take appropriate steps to protect them from inappropriate conduct.
35. Fairness: be fair in competitive situations, selecting a team, disciplinary issues, and all other matters; and be open-minded and willing to listen and learn.

CARING

36. Safe Competition: put safety and health considerations above the desire to win; never permit student-athletes to intentionally injure any player or engage in reckless behavior that might cause injury to themselves or others.

37. Caring Environment: consistently demonstrate concern for student-athletes as individuals and encourage them to look out for one another and think and act as a team.

CITIZENSHIP

38. Honor the Spirit of Rules: observe and require student-athletes to observe the spirit and the letter of all rules including the rules of the game and those relating to eligibility, recruitment, transfers, practices, and other provisions regulating interscholastic competition.
39. Improper Gamesmanship: promote sportsmanship over gamesmanship; don't cheat; resist temptations to gain competitive advantage through strategies or techniques (such as devious rule violations, alteration of equipment or the field of play, or tactics designed primarily to induce injury or fear of injury) that violate the rules, disrespect the highest traditions of the sport, or change the nature of competition by practices that negate or diminish the impact of the core athletic skills that define the sport.

I have read and understand the requirements of this Code of Conduct. I will act in accord with this Code. I understand that school (and district) officials as well as league and section officials will and should expect that I will follow this Code.

Teacher-Coach Signature _____

Date _____

Excerpted from the California Interscholastic Federation.

Index